RUSSIA:
Yesterday, Today, Tomorrow

Voice of the Young Generation

Editors:
Victor Pavlenkov, Peter Pappas

FC-Izdat
1996

Victor Pavlenkov, Peter Pappas

RUSSIA: YESTERDAY, TODAY, TOMORROW
Voice of the young generation

Copyright © by FC-Izdat

Library of Congress Catalog Card Number: 96-061435
ISBN 0-9637035-5-2

Published by FC-Izdat,
USA-Russia

Printed in the USA
Artwork by Bob Gale

In memory of
Vladlen and Igor Pavlenkov

Valdlen Pavlenkov. Nizhny Novgorod. 1950

CONTENTS

Introduction

One day in October 1994, I stood at *Out of Town News*, the international magazine and newspaper kiosk in the middle of Harvard Square, leafing through the Russian language newspapers.

In one of the newspapers – I seem to recall that it was *The Moscow News* – I read a small article, which claimed that according to a recently conducted sociological poll among high school students in Moscow, the most prestigious profession among girls was held to be that of high-class prostitute, and the boys were even in assigning their preference to commerce and organized crime as the most popular career choices. I had seen similar articles in the press before, but the matter-of-fact tone of the article really disturbed me this time. I bought the paper, and after reading it in a nearby cafe, threw it in the trash and went home.

Over the next few days, however, I could not get rid of the bitter aftertaste the article had left me with. I kept imagining crew-cuts above the hostile glares of the boys and the heavily rouged faces of Russian beauties on some Russian version of Sunset Boulevard – Pushkin Square in Moscow, for example. And what about the "Russian boys" of Dostoevsky? What has become of them, the few who ask the eternal questions, the "fair youth with burning eyes?" What statistical niche is allotted them now? Indeed, do they exist at all any longer?

I kept remembering the kitchens of the seventies: long conversations and discussions nightly, secret readings of underground literature, self-published (with a high degree of risk) magazines and with sudden urgency, I decided to try to find out just who they are, this new generation of Russians. Hence, the beginning of the project **Russia: Yesterday, Today, Tomorrow**, the results of which are presented in this book.

The project was implemented in Nizhny Novgorod[1] and Boston by **Pavlenkov Memorial**, an organization I created to perpetuate the ideas and the deeds of my father – Vladlen Pavlenkov.

---

[1] Nizhny Novgorod, formerly Gorky, is the third largest city in Russia with a population of 1.5 million people. In recent years, Moscow and St. Petersburg became gateways to Russia for foreign investors and major Western corporations and saw dramatic increases in real estate values, food prices, salaries and so on. Nizhny Novgorod remains more representative of the rest of Russia, for the most part untouched by Western influence.

On the other hand, recent changes initiated by Governor Boris Nemtsov, the renowned reformist, have transformed Nizhny Novgorod from "a closed city" to the city with the most progressive local administration in the country. So, while Nizhny Novgorod experiences the same scope of problems (the slowing down of industrial output, massive layoffs) which plague all of Russia during the post-communist transition, its identity as a major Central Russian city with a reform-oriented administration puts it in a unique position to reflect the processes taking place in Russia now.

Vladlen Pavlenkov, a former history teacher, Soviet political prisoner, writer, and expert on international postal communications, died on January 31, 1990, in Jersey City, NJ. He was born May 4, 1929, in Nizhny Novgorod, USSR, and was named after the founder of the USSR (Vladlen is an abbreviation of Vladimir Lenin). However, his nickname was Volya, which in Russian means both "willpower" and "freedom," and throughout his life he came to epitomize both. After graduating from Gorky University in 1951, he taught history in colleges and high schools in Germany and Gorky.

His career was cut short on October 3, 1969, with his arrest and subsequent conviction on charges of "anti-Soviet propaganda and agitation." The charges included authorship of a book entitled *2+2=4*, which attempted to provide common sense answers to Soviet economic problems. Despite KGB pressure, he refused to confess or recant and was given the maximum sentence: seven years in a labor camp.

After being forced to emigrate, he came to the US in November 1979. In 1982, he founded a nonprofit organization, **Freedom of Communications**, the goal of which was to promote free and private communication between people in the USSR and the outside world.

Through the dedicated and tireless work of its founder, FC initiated and saw approved nine amendments to the Universal Postal Union Congress Constitution, designed to improve international postal communications. He frequently testified in Congress on postal matters, published newsletters and brochures with advice for mailers to the USSR, and collected and documented examples of Soviet postal interference. After

11

his death, his family received a large number of letters from throughout the world. But the real honor was a **Tribute to Vladlen K. Pavlenkov, Congressional Record – Senate, S 1391 – S 1392, February 21, 1990**[2]. In a letter to his widow, Carl Gershman, President of the National Endowment for Democracy, wrote:

"... Vladlen was a man of deep convictions, who fought persistently and tenaciously for his ideals. I believe that the world is a better, more open and more peaceful place as a result of his tireless efforts and devotion to the cause of freedom."

My father believed in small things. Seven years later to the day of his initial imprisonment, at 6:00 a.m., a KGB car dropped him off at our front door. I immediately began questioning him about his political views, his personal beliefs, philosophy, etc. He smiled evasively and joked with me. He had just become a free man again after all; but later that evening he yielded to my persistent queries.

To make a small, but *real* contribution toward the improvement of people's lives, that was his goal. That was the wisdom he imparted to his son after seven long years. I remember being somewhat disappointed. This prosaic philosophy seemed petty to me in comparison to the great visions of revolutions, sedition, grandiose doctrines and political power plays which were filling my head at the time. It took a long time for me to realize the simple beauty of those words, even though I was presented with examples almost immediately.

---

[2] Speech by Senator Diconsini

One of the first projects he undertook concerned the redemption of bottles and cans in our neighborhood in Gorky. By law, every store which sold the products in glassware had to provide for the redemption of such glassware. But the local supermarket had closed its redemption center and all the locals had to carry bags full of empty glass to other neighborhoods. After a long trail of letters and intense negotiations in our kitchen with the supermarket's management and representatives of The Ministry of Commerce from Moscow, the solution was found–a redemption truck started making a regular route in our neighborhood.

There are many more examples of similar undertakings, the most significant of them being **Freedom of Communications**. It is in his memory that the project of *Russia: Yesterday, Today and Tomorrow* was implemented. A small glimpse of a small group in a large city in the world's largest country.

A few years ago the importance of Russia and its fate would command the front pages of leading newspapers. Russia was a question mark in the story of modern civilization, a major player in the game of world power. Now, as it undergoes tumultuous times, its population and sphere of interest reduced to a fraction of its previous mighty size, it mostly resides on the back pages, its place there assured by the intensity of its border conflicts. And yet the uniqueness of the Russian experience, especially in the last century, draws our attention, and we struggle to comprehend the intensity and the scale of questions Russia has faced and attempted to ask. Values held as fundamental by an over-

13

whelming majority of the world were thrown into question, examined, and then rejected by generations of new Soviet citizens. Total equality and justice were pronounced as the predominant goals of the new social order. This ability to abandon the *baggage of the centuries*, and boldly plunge into the unknown despite enormous sacrifice was daring, indeed.

And now, with these experiments having failed miserably, the world can evaluate and reevaluate the rich data left behind for us. But the country which performed this feat, which took it upon itself to build communism (and dearly, oh how dearly, paid for it), is still there.

It is this very recent transition period in Russian history, encompassing the plunge from a strict authoritarian regime to the relative anarchy of unknown social formations we call post-communism, which, we feel, allows us to have at least a small positive impact, while affording us a cultural snapshot, if you will, of a generation truly on the cutting edge of democracy.

And so, it was with the hopes of achieving the above mentioned goals, that **Pavlenkov Memorial** held an **essay** competition among high school seniors in Nizhny Novgorod, formerly Gorky, on the topic: **"Russia: Yesterday, Today, Tomorrow"**

Submitted essays were collected and judged by a jury. Prizes were awarded to the winners. Selected essays were to be published in Russia in a book, together with a review of the essays and the results of a questionnaire. An English version of the book with translations of the essays is to be distributed among educational and cultural institutions in the USA and Russia.

Designed to accompany the essay competition, a sociological survey was conducted through the distribution of **questionnaires** to the participants. The questionnaire was developed by Dr. Alexander Babyonishev of Harvard University, one of the principals of the project. The survey was based on the "indirect method" of questioning designed to gain an understanding of the attitudes of young Russians toward Russian history and recent reforms.

The project had the following goals:

Humanitarian . The project is designed to help preserve and sustain the humanitarian traditions of Russia among the upcoming generation in Nizhny Novgorod. Russia now is undergoing a tumultuous period in its history. The degree of uncertainty brought about by unexpected and radical changes is dangerously high, threatening the most important traditions of culture and education, the very traditions which helped Russian culture survive during the years of communist repression.

We believe that promoting and rewarding writing and self-expression among the upcoming generation of Russian youth helps to maintain cultural continuity in the uncertain climate of Russia today.

Informational . The collection of essays and questionnaires will comprise a unique body of material – the signature of a generation which entered schools under the hegemony of communist ideas and is graduating and entering the real world in the post-communist era.

Educational . This book, with the top twenty prize-winning essays, and its corresponding English edition, as well as an analysis of the collected essays and questionnaires, will be distributed among educational and cultural institutions in the USA, and will provide readers with an insightful view of the problems, prospects and aspirations of the new generation of today's Russia.

What I wanted my Russian counterparts to do were three things: advertise solicitations for the essay competition, while describing the prize-fund, collect the essays and questionnaires, and send them to us. Simple enough it would seem, but this was made difficult and trying by the bureaucratic obstacles placed in our path. There were others, but one illustration of an obstacle to be patiently overcome should suffice.

While the tasks seemed to be simple enough, their implementation and the task of receiving a letter from the Governor of Nizhny proved to be riddled with numerous obstacles and difficulties, multiplied by the noise of old phone-lines of a relatively reliable, if expensive, voice connection.

In Russia, currently, every fax has to be registered with a phone company, which requires quite a hefty registration fee. Rumor has it that there are *fax-catchers,* who search for and levy heavy fines on the users of unregistered faxes.

(I imagine the stern faces of a group of fax-catchers, assembled in darkness at an ordinary looking shed in a rundown neighborhood of Nizhny, waiting to intercept an unregistered fax transmission. Tension hangs thickly in the darkness, as all intently wait for the signal from a grungy looking guy by the interception apparatus, week-old growth on his face, having been here, on a stakeout, all that time.

Suddenly, he gives a sign to be quiet, and all movements and sounds cease. "Third entrance, seventh floor!" His commands are short, precise, given out in one breath. As the men pour out the door, checking their gear for the last time, one stops in a doorway, turns to face the technical guy for the last time, and says with a glimpse of a smile on his rough face: "Good job, bro!"

Darkness, just the sound of breathing and stealthy footsteps. At the end of a dark corridor you see a vertical strip of light which, as the sound of breathing and footsteps approach, starts flying away in a whirl of boomeranging rotation, turning into the swirling rainbow of a roulette wheel... Large letters on the screen: FIGHT THE TEMPTATION OF UNREGISTERED FAXATION!!!)

So, with the number of faxes being so limited in Nizhny, some preliminary information was transferred over the phone to my cousin, Ira Pavlenkov. Then, I was given a fax number at my relative's office, which proved to be inaccessible. Somewhat frustrated by the slow pace, I tried another number. I knew this person from before, when he came to Boston, looking for opportunities. Having helped him before, I expected some cooperation in return, but the premise turned out to be false, when, after having made fifteen calls, and finally connecting and transmitting the fax, my friend found out the next day that it was thrown out by his secretary. That was probably the lowest point of the project: alone on the other side of the ocean, I was unable to secure anything more than verbal agreements, while the work had not even been started yet. But at that point Katya Goryunova, after my pleas from abroad took it upon herself to make sure that project was done, arranging for a reliable fax, delivering the papers back and forth and becoming a liaison between us and the governor's office, and performing other necessary tasks.

Finally, in December 1994 and in January 1995 we ran the following announcement in Nizhny's newspapers, as well as on radio and TV. Here is the translation of it:

Vladlen Pavlenkov Memorial Trust announces an essay competition among high school seniors in Nizhny Novgorod. The topic shall be:

"Russia: Yesterday, Today, Tomorrow"
Conditions:

1. Length. Ten to twenty hand-written pages, maximum 24 pages, based on the size of a standard Russian notebook.

2. Submission terms.

a. Submit essays by February 1, 1995 at the teachers' room at Lyceum #40 (formerly school #40)

b. Include name, school, phone number, or address at which the student can be contacted.

c. Name and address should be on a special sheet so that it is not visible to the jurors.

3. Judgment guidelines. Originality, logic of the composition, grammar, and the personal discretion of members of the jury .

4. Jury membership. Jury membership is confidential, but the jury is made up of qualified professionals from Russia and the USA.

Prizes.

1. First place - A computer system with a printer.

2. Second to fifth places - typewriters.

3. Sixth to tenth places - Dictaphone.

4. Eleventh to twentieth - Yearly subscription to a Russian literary magazine.

Submitted essays become the property of the Fund. Selected essays will be translated into English and published in a book which will be distributed among educational institutions. Therefore, authors are advised to include their address in case the aforementioned institutions would like to contact the authors. All contributors whose essays are included in the book will receive a complimentary copy.

In the organization and implementation of the commitments made by us, we have received help from many people, without whom this project could not have been completed. On the Russian side: Katya Goryunova, Olga Harlamova and Ira Pavlenkova. On the US side: Russ Buckley, Peter Pappas, Eugene Jones as well as John and Madeline Carney, who were our major financial contributors.

By phone conversations, I secured a promise of cooperation from the School-Lyceum #40 (all high schools are still known by their numbers in Russia), namely from the vice-principal David Erenkrants, a math teacher, who collected and sent us the essays with a visiting teacher from Connecticut.

Finally, the essays and completed questionnaires were in my hands, and I was looking at a small box, containing forty three essays – two pounds of paper. The majority of the essays are in school notebooks, within covers of different colors, while a few are written on legal-size paper. What do they hold within? And who are they, the contributors, who trusted an ad, decided to write and carried their resolution to completion. Below are the names of the participants:

Orlov, Vasily, school #30
Tetelkin, Evgeny, school #51
Gushin, Mikhail, school #40,

19

Shmakov, Dmitry, school #91,
Holina, Kseniya, school #30,
Dobrohotov, Vladimir, school #40
Trubitsina, Irina, school #40
Podnebesny, Andrey, school #33,
Chegin, Dmitry, school #126
Bandakov, Pavel, school #14.
Maksimov, Ivan, school #180
Tuhsanova, Elizaveta, school #404
Bodrievskaya, Irina, school #405
Glazunov, Alexander, school #40
Koroteeva, Irina, school #30,
Marinin, Sergey, school #30,
Bityurina, Ekaterina, school #70
Chernevskij, Artyom, school #40
Osokin, Maksim, school #40,
Vereshagin, Egor, school #25
Lapshin, Sergey, school #40,
Malkin. Andrey, school #40,
Miroshnik, Oksana, school #54,
Lebedev, Evgeny, school #7,
Platonova, Arina, school #40
Belova, Olga, school #30
Derigeeva, Anna, school #25
Porubkin, Dmitry, school #160,
Vidyaeva, Elena, school #7,
Chelnokov, Evgeny, school #40
Kalaeva, Irina, school #7
Soldunova, Tatyana, school #7
Batasheva, Tatyana, school #7
Gabinet, Natalya, school #7,
Soldatova, Anna, school #30
Ezhov, Mikhail, school #35
Kukanova, Marina, school #84
Grigoryeva, Irina, school #13
Bak, Yuliya, school #40
Guseva, Yuliya, school #25
Glushaeva, Svetlana, school #25
Shitova, Olga, school #40

At this point, the essays were distributed to the judges:
Alexander Babyonishev, historian and demographer; Aleksey

Rozenvain, a teacher from Kiev; Svetlana Pavlenkov, former lecturer at Gorky University; and Mikhail Gershtein, a scientist. The grades were calculated and the prizes assigned. The questionnaires were analyzed and comprise a separate chapter in the book, which will include a number of essays translated into English together with a synopsis of major events and ideas of Russia's history and culture. The book taken as a whole should provide a glimpse at contemporary Russia and its history, an appropriate introduction for interested young scholars of all ages and grade levels.

Here, I want to mention briefly the financing of the entire project. Initially, I invested a lot of time and money in preparing a professional proposal, which included, besides the plan and the description of the project and a lot of background information, a letter from Nizhny' governor, Boris Nemtsov, who welcomed the project. The proposal was distributed to sixty foundations and corporations, who do business in Russia. I followed up with phone calls, follow-up letters and so on. Not a single positive response. NOTHING! Of course, the failure to secure any financial help had its negative effect on me, but the inspiring memory of my father, who paid for his ideas and beliefs and was often left on his own to carry out his projects, to see them to completion, has helped me not to stumble.

At the presentation in School #40 in Nizhny Novgorod, when we distributed the promised prizes to the winners (Orlov and Tetelkin received laptop computers; Shmakov, Gushin and Holina, typewriters; the rest, dictaphones, subscriptions, and

21

Parker pens). I emphasized that all of it – the project, the prizes, the upcoming book – is a part of a spiritual legacy left by Vladlen Pavlenkov.

The project received a very positive response in Nizhny Novgorod. The presentation was featured on TV, newspapers, radio. Some participants said that writing the essay helped them in sorting out their thoughts, in choosing the direction of their education. While we were asked and encouraged to continue the essay competitions on a regular basis, only time will show if we can make the commitment both financially and time-wise. At the very end, I would like to thank my wife, Eileen Carney and my children, Volya and Elena, for enduring the strain and burden of mixed-up schedules, of my trips to Russia, of turning the house into an editorial office and so on. Eileen's generous support and dedication to the project were invaluable. Also, I can not fail to mention my dear friends and partners: Marsha and Alan Rosenoff, who would open their doors to me at any hour and were the very first to purchase this book.

The readers of this book will judge for themselves what we have achieved in this project. The book contains 20 essays (unfortunately, the constraints of the volume do not allow us to print all of the essays) and the results of the survey. Again, this is a snapshot of a transitional generation of Russia, in 1995. To conclude, this book is a collection of the thoughts and emotions of Russia's youth, of those who will live and work in Russia, of those, who will determine Russia's future, and of the legacies of the past which they have inherited.

Below are photographs of some of the essayists at the meeting in Nizhny Novgorod in November 1995.

From left to right: Egor Vereshagin, Vasily Orlov, Olga Belova, Irina Koroteeva, Kseniya Holina, Irina Bodrievskaya

From left to right: Oksana Miroshnik, Egor Vereshagin, Elizaveta Tuhsanova, Vladimir Dobrohotov, Vasily Orlov

CHRONOLOGY

862 AD – Viking family of Rurik takes over Novgorod, a northern Slavic city, establishing the dynasty which will last until the 16th century. Rus', or Russia, as the country came to be known, was located on the way from Scandinavia to Byzantium (Constantinople), which at that point in time was a major economic and political power. The legend that Rurik was **summoned** to Novgorod to rule, persists in Russian mythology until today.

863-885 – Two Byzantine monks, Cyril and Methodius create the first Slavic written language (Cyrillic alphabet)

882 – Oleg, a Rurik-successor, captures Kiev and makes it the capital of Rus'.

907 – Oleg conducts an expedition, conquering Constantinople

941 – Rurik's son, Igor, who succeeded Oleg, conducts a raid on Constantinople

957 – Olga, Igor's wife, who succeeded him, is baptized

989 – conversion of the Russians from Slavonic paganism to Byzantine Christianity by Vladimir. Faced with the necessity of adopting a monotheistic religion for the unification of his people, Vladimir pondered Catholicism, Judaism, Islam and Byzantine Orthodoxy. According to the legend, Catholicism was rejected because of its "gloominess", Judaism – because Jews had no home, Islam – because of its prohibition of alcohol. Churches in Byzantium were so magnificent that the ambassadors of Vladimir felt in Heaven inside them. Along with the new religion came Byzantine culture which the young Russian culture absorbed intensely. Churches and new houses were built. Many Greek books were translated. Chronicles were written.

1030 AD – First school is started in Novgorod by Yaroslav "The Wise" (1019-1054)

1054-1073 – Russkaya Pravda (Russian Truth), first Russian code of laws, is written.

1147 – First mention of Moscow in a chronicle

1221 – Nizhny Novgorod is founded

1237-1240 – Mongolian invasion under the leadership of Baty Khan (grandson of Genghiz). Kiev falls in 1240.

1240 – Alexander Nevsky, prince of Novgorod, defeats invading Swedes on the Neva

1242 – Alexander Nevsky defeats the German Order on Lake Peipus. He later travels to Mongolia to see the Khan and dies on the way back. His descendants were to become Muscovite princes.

1237-1480 – The Mongolian Yoke. Mongolian domination during this period separated Russia from the rest of the world and left its legacy forever in the formation of national character. A weakened Russia was also attacked on the West by Germans and Lithuanians, separating Kievan Rus' into Western and Eastern parts. This period sees the emergence of Moscow as a major principality under the rule of Ivan I Kalita (1328-1340), who rose to prominence by collecting large tributes from the rest of Russia for the Mongols. It was his grandson, Dmitry Donskoy (1359-1389), who was able to achieve the first military victory over the Tartar/Mongol forces at Kulikov Field in command of unified Russian troops.

1326 – Seat of church Metropolitan transferred to Moscow

1380 – The first major military defeat of Tartar/Mongol forces at Kulikov Field by Dmitry Donskoy

1382 – Moscow is burned by Tokhtamysh, ensuring a century of continuing, if waning dominance by Mongols

1453 – Capture of Byzantium (Constantinople) by the Ottoman Turks. Russia remains the major Orthodox power.

1472 – Marriage of Ivan III (1462-1505) to Sofia Palaeologa, niece of the last Byzantine emperor. The legacy of Byzantine Orthodox Christianity would lead towards the establishment of the idea of Moscow being "The Third Rome."

1478 – Incorporation of Novgorod into Moscovy by Ivan III, marking the end of Novgorod as a democratic republic which had a general assembly – the *Veche*, and whose trade missions established Russian cities as far as the Urals.

1480 – Ivan III ends tributes to the Khans. Mongols come to Russia, but leave without engaging Russian troops at the river Ugra. At the beginning of the Mongol Yoke, Russia consisted of a large number of principalities often at war with one another, after the era of Mongol domination, Russia is a unified country under the leadership of Moscow.

1485-1516 – Construction of a new Kremlin in Moscow

1547-1584 – Ivan IV ("The Terrible"). The reign of Ivan IV saw Russia defeat its traditional enemies, the Tartars, on the Volga (Kazan and Astrakhan), wage wars against Poland and Sweden for possession of the Baltic, expand to the Urals and Siberia, and fortify its southern frontiers with establishment of the Cossacks. It was also a reign of terror and of the establishment

of absolute power with the help of a special police force –
oprichniki. In a fit of rage, Ivan IV killed his own son in 1582.
The "Times of Troubles" (*Smuta*) were to follow.

1558 - 1583 – Livonian War against Poland and Sweden
1564 – First book printed in Moscow
1565-1572 – The reign of terror (*oprichnina*)
1570 – Ivan "The Terrible"'s pogrom of Novgorod
1581 – Yermak's expedition begins the conquest of Siberia

1601-1613 – The "Times of Trouble" (*Smuta*). Ivan IV's last
son, the feeble-minded Fyodor, inherited the crown in 1584.
But it was his brother-in-law, Boris Godunov, who ruled until
his death in 1598. Fyodor was the last Rurik on the Russian
throne. Boris Godunov became a first elected tsar in 1598.
1598-1605 – Boris Godunov's reign was marked by major
famines and the appearances of the self-declared sons of Ivan
with a claim to the throne supported by the Polish army, the
Cossacks, and some nobility. Boris Godunov also institutes a
system of serfdom, contributing to the unrest among peasants.
1601-1604 – Famines
1606-1607 – Peasants revolt under the leadership of Bolotnikov
1610-1612 – Poles occupy Moscow
1612-1613 – Nizhny Novgorod's popular militia headed by
Minin and Pozharsky frees Moscow from Poles. Poles are defeated as Cossacks side with militia.
1613 – Mikhail Romanov is elected Tsar (Caesar) by Land
Assembly. The Romanov dynasty would rule Russia for the
next 304 years.
1649 – *Ulozhenie*, a Law Code which legalizes serfdom
1652 – Nikon becomes church patriarch and immediately sets
out to reform Russian Orthodoxy in order to bring Orthodox rituals to uniform code. While the reforms were mostly concerned
with rituals, they were fanatically opposed by large parts of the
population, who came to be known as "Old Believers", and who
viewed the reforms as a sign of foreign influence. They were
severely persecuted, whole villages were burned. Their leader,
the monk Avvakum was burned alive. This schism, known as
Raskol (Split) alienated a large part of the Russian population
and persists in the church today.
1670-1671 – Revolt of Sten'ka Razin. Protesting the heavy
taxes on his booty from the Caspian Sea, Sten'ka and his
Cossacks deposed the governor of Astrakhan'. His revolt
proved popular with the unhappy peasants but crumbled under

26

the pressures of fighting the regular army. Sten'ka Razin was publicly beheaded on Red Square in Moscow.

1689-1725 – Peter The Great, grandson of Mikhail Romanov. Peter's push toward progress and westernization was achieved through the creation of a military-industrial complex out of the country. Peter's opening to the West was achieved by military victories in the Great Northern War (1700-1721) with Sweden, and by the establishment of a new capital in St. Petersburg. The creation of the Russian Navy (1695) and subsequent conquests in the Far East made Russia a world power. Peter brought education, the establishment of legal law, and encouraged contact with the West and the immigration of Europeans.

1725 – Academy of Science is founded

1755 – Moscow University is founded by Mikhail Lomonosov, who is considered a founder of Russian science

1762-1796 – Catherine The Great. A German princess on the Russian throne, she treated men as kings treat their mistresses and oversaw a major expansion of Russian borders, consolidating the western push by Peter. From colonization of Alaska (1784), to the incorporation of Crimea (1783) and Ukraine (1786), and through three partitions of Poland (1772-1795), Russia conducted many wars in their push to the West and South. At the same time Catherine continued a tradition of inviting the immigration of foreigners, and the development of science and education.

1772-1774 – Revolt of Pugachev.

1787-1792 – Wars with the Turks

1801-1825 – Alexander I, grandson of Catherine. During his reign a proposal for constitutional monarchy and the reform of serfdom was drafted by his minister, Speransky, but never brought forward.

1812 – Napoleon's failed invasion. Battle of Borodino. The burning of Moscow by Russians. Napoleon's retreat which ends with Russian troops occupying Paris in 1814.

1817 – Nizhny Novgorod Fair is established

1817-1864 – Caucasus War. Russia conquers Caucasus in a bloody and costly war as it battles for domination of the region.

1819 – University founded in St. Petersburg

1825 – Decembrists' uprising after the death of Alexander I by army officers and intellectuals. The Decembrists are considered the forefathers of the revolutionary movement.

1825-1855 – Considered a reactionary, Nicholas I saw his country undergo industrialization and the creation of the powerful social stratum of intelligentsia. The Crimean War (1853-1856) underscored the weaknesses of serfdom-based economy.
1855-1881 – Alexander II. This tsar ended the unsuccessful Crimean War and completed the conquest of the Caucasus (1859). He also oversaw the abolition of serfdom (1861) and far-reaching judicial reforms, only to be assassinated by the revolutionaries who preached terrorism. (1881) While the abolition of serfdom released a peasant from a noble's ownership, the peasants were left in communes (*obshina*) with no individual ownership of land. This period also sees a strong, organized revolutionary movement by part of the intelligentsia, expansion to the East, taking over Middle Asia, and the occupation of Manchuria.
1894-1917 – Nicholas II, the last tsar.
1904-1905 – Russo-Japanese War
1905 – Revolution of 1905
1906 – First Duma
1906-1911 – Prime minister Stolypin puts down a revolution with hangings and institutes land reforms aimed at the dissolution of *obshina* and at populating Siberia and Kazakhstan. He is assassinated by a revolutionary and his reforms fail.
1914 – World War I starts.
1917 – February revolution. Abdication of Nicholas II. October revolution by Bolsheviks under the leadership of Lenin.
1917 – Establishment of Cheka (Secret Police)
1918 – Murder of Tsar and his family. Peace treaty between Russia and Germany.
1918-1920 – Civil War. Bolsheviks consolidate power, fighting peasant revolts, and White armies. They practice a policy of War Communism, resulting in famine and mass executions.
1921 – New Economic Policy (NEP) begins, as central government frees the restrictions on trade and gives peasants the land.

1924 – With Lenin's death, Stalin slowly takes over the power.
1929 – End of NEP. Industrialization and collectivization begins. Collectivization forces peasants into kolhoz (collective), over which the government has total control, using state enforced famine (1931-1933), which resulted in the loss of 9 million peasants. Industrialization was based on forced labor of prisoners.

1930-s – Mass terror practiced by Stalin's secret police.
1934 – Nizhny Novgorod is renamed Gorky in honor of the revolutionary writer.
1936-1938 – Mass execution of Soviet Army commanders, show trials of Zinovyev, Bukharin, et al.
1939-1940 – Molotov-Ribentropp peace treaty between USSR and Germany. Russia occupies Eastern Poland and Baltic states.
1941 – 1945 – Great Patriotic War with Hitler's Germany. USSR looses 27 million people. Victorious conclusion of the war allowed Stalin to occupy Eastern Europe as was agreed at the Yalta Conference (1945) with Roosevelt and Churchill.
1946 – Beginning of the Cold War. USSR sets up puppet governments in Eastern Europe and organizes Warsaw Pact.
1953 – Death of Stalin. Execution of Beria (Chief of Secret Police).

1954 – Process of amnesty for political prisoners and the beginning of political and cultural thaw.
1956 – 20th Party Congress. Khrushchev denounces Stalin's cult of personality. Hungarian revolution quashed.
1959 – Khrushchev visits USA
1961 – Yuri Gagarin is a first man in space
1962 – Worker protests against price increases is put down in execution style in Novocherkassks
1964 – Khrushchev ousted

1964-1982 – Leonid Brezhnev rules the country in what later would be described as the "years of stagnation".
1966 – Sinyavsky and Daniel political trial for publishing abroad is the beginning of the confrontation between the KGB and the dissident movement
1968 – Soviet occupation of Czechoslovakia
1971 – Solzhenitsin, a writer who became known for his description of labor camps during Stalin's time, is deported from USSR
1975 – Sakharov, a nuclear scientist who became an outspoken human rights activist wins Nobel Peace Prize.
1979 – Soviet invasion of Afghanistan.
1980 – Sakharov exiled to Gorky

1985 – New leader, Gorbachev calls for *perestroika*.
1986 – US/Soviet summit in Reykjavik (Regan and Gorbachev). Amnesty of political prisoners begins. Nuclear disaster at Chernobyl.

1987 – Sakharov released from exile.
1988 – Ethnic unrest begins in the Caucasus, the Baltics and Middle Asia
1989 – Yeltsin and Sakharov elected to Parliament. Soviet troops pull out of Afghanistan. General strikes of miners. Berlin Wall comes down. Warsaw Pact is disbanded.
1990 – Yeltsin resigns from Communist Party.
1991 – Yeltsin becomes first democratically elected Russian President.
1991 – August Coup by Communist renegades. Yeltsin, a defiant Russian President, barricades himself in the Parliament building – the White House, with a leader of Parliament - Hazbulatov and Vice-President Rutskoy. Yeltsin emerges triumphant after three tense days. (One of the people who spend this time with Yeltsin is Boris Nemtsov, a representative from Gorky. He later becomes governor of the Nizhny region as the city is given its original name of Nizhny Novgorod.) Yeltsin disbands the Communist Party and retires Gorbachev. At a meeting with Ukrainian and Belorussian, leaders Yeltsin disbands the Soviet Union, and former Soviet republics become independent states.
1992 – Privatization begins with issues of vouchers. Prices are freed as inflation reaches 1000%. Treaties on the recognition and security with former republics are signed. Organized crime penetrates the economy as the Soviet management apparatus crumbles.
1993 – Yeltsin disbands Congress and orders troops to bomb and storm the White House, arresting Rutskoy and Hazbulatov. Election of the first State Duma. Referendum on reforms and new constitution passes and new Russian Constitution becomes law.
1994 – Russian troops are sent in Chechnya as Russia tries to maintain its hold on the Caucasus.
1995 – The war with Chechnya intensifies, as Chechens conduct raids into Russian territory and take hostages. Communists win in Duma elections.
1996 – Yeltsin narrowly wins elections, with Communists coming in a strong second place, as he promises the end of war in Chechnya. A strong third runner-up, Lebed, wins a place in the Yeltsin government. As Yeltsin suffers from serious health problems, Chechens retake the capital - Grozny. Lebed is sent as an emissary to Chechnya and brokers a peace plan.

Russia: Yesterday, Today, Tomorrow

Essays

Views of Nizhny Novgorod's Kremlin

ГОРЬКИЙ

Bak, Yuliya

RUSSIA: A FATE TO BE CHOSEN

"Growing tired of meaningless and overtaxing 'running in place', a nation may throw itself to extremes if only to interrupt the tragicomic experiment of wingless reformism."

A.S. Panarin

The Soviet socialist order, which wiped out almost all of the socio-economic traditions and mentality of Russia, has itself disappeared into non-existence.

For a period of seventy years the country found itself under the heel of a totalitarian regime. "I know no other country where men can breathe so freely," are words written by the poet Isakovsky during the pinnacle of mass-repression. Lies, fear, violence, and slave labor – these were the conditions which determined people's lives. Meanwhile, red flags and the portraits of beloved leaders were grandly displayed everywhere, patriotic slogans fluttered in the air.

A few generations of cheated peoples at first believed in, and subsequently lost faith in the victory of communism.

Industrialization, collectivization, victory in the great patriotic war, post-war reconstruction, agricultural expansion in the frontier, and the era of the conquest of outer space – these were the monumental stepping stones of the Russian nation. These accomplishments were accompanied by gigantic human, ecological, and energy expenditures; sacrifices which could only have been made with limitless faith in the triumph of illusory ideals, which the communists had hypnotized the Russian people into accepting. Many of the great achievements of the Soviet people were attained through the forced-labor of innocent prisoners.

However, the utopianism of the initial ideological guidelines brought about the inflation of ideals, the demoralization of the people, by the ever-growing lies of the party-government nomenclature, slowed industrial and scientific development; generated a duplicitous rendering of Russian life in Soviet art, and, as a consequence, led to the full degradation of the society.

And now, this great, millions-strong Russian superpower, and centuries-old cultural tradition, is again faced with a choice of historic proportions. The fates of the Russian peoples, from the intelligentsia to the ruling elite and business circles; the paths of economic and cultural development; and the country's stature on the Eurasian continent are intertwined in a dense knot of contradiction.

Where to..., who will Russia follow? This question painfully confronts government and the society as a whole, since the choice of the path of development embodies great risk in its direct consequences, which are matters of life and death.

In August of 1991, the country parted with old illusions. The party-government ruling elite realized the state of the world-

34

wide bankruptcy of socialism. The nation has entered into the unknown. The new rulers of the country, walking the path of changes in structure and means of production, have created conditions for the appearance of a new ruling class.

This new ruling class has positions of command in the political structure and, more importantly, in the economy. They have no real opposition.

As a consequence, mass-consciousness is discrediting entrepreneurial economic initiative, and democratic politics. Thus begins the demoralization of the people who lack any real choices, or alternatives.

Such exploitation of democratic values, by the forces of old, creates, in the opinion of A.S. Panarin, a situation of so-called "deferred risk", which is capable of debilitating reform as a whole, and is more fundamental, and more unpredictable, than political coups, which only effect the interests of the narrow circles of the ruling elite.

An analogous situation is taking place in the political arena: no one is willing to take a risk. The strategy for immediate success forces politicians to conform, to engage in plagiarism in the fields of ideas, slogans, and programs. As a result, instead of a rich political spectrum, which can offer the people a real variety of choice, there is a homogenous political climate.

Having lost all hope of finding persistent and honest reformers, among the existing leaders, the people are prone to rebellion against the newly formed political class. This threatens the loss of any historic or cultural legacy.

Following the logic of capitalist development, it is possible to guess that, in the not-so-distant future of Russia, the nomenclature of capitalists, who have received their inheritance, together with the power structure, will be replaced by a new generation, which would have no governmental backing. This new generation would have to be different, having absorbed the qualities of true free enterprise. The rotation of the entrepreneurial elite will take place in the spirit of a "populist capitalism", with its characteristic tendency toward thrift, and an unacceptance of unbridled spending, connected with leisure time, artistic pursuits and donation. With such development, the country approaches a clash between the entrepreneurial sector (meshanstvo) and the intelligentsia. The self-made representatives of this populist capitalism, having no obligation to the former power structure, would not be inclined to finance the expenditures of the intelligentsia in the organization of funds and clubs of all kinds, which was undertaken by the representative capitalist nomenclature, in order to launder the party's assets. Moreover, a negative reaction to social programs, to the creation of cultural centers, and to social support for the unprotected layers of the population, could be expected from this class.

In this struggle between the two capitalist sides (the nomenclature and populist capitalists), the intelligentsia, losing the financial support of the latter, is inclined to support the former. Here, we need to underscore the importance of the spiritual fundamentals in the establishment of new social groups, new processes, and new relations. A lack of spiritual culture, and the loss of spiritual legitimacy, by any given social group, dooms it to social isolation, its loss of social stature, and, as a consequence, leads to its demise. Today the loss of spiritual legitimacy threatens numerous groups of professionals/specialists, who, demonstrating political conservatism and nostalgia for the past, and rejecting profane forms of market enterprise, have nevertheless preserved certain basic values of industriousness, discipline, and organization., without which a productive economy is impossible. A particular sector of the intelligentsia, however, which is sympathetic to a certain degree of education and an inclination towards charitable action by the representatives of the nomenclature capitalism, saw in the mindset and behavior of these disenchanted layers of the population a rejection of progress by these "backward people".

This blindness of the intelligentsia, which refuses to acknowledge today's realities, shows itself in all cases in which its favorites, carrying these advance teachings, gain the helm of power. The Bolsheviks played the role of these "carriers" in their era. The intellectuals, both Russian and western, who were sympathetic to their global experiment involving "the people", preferred not to notice the accompanying "costs" of the horrible famine of 1933, the Gulag system, etc. In our time, this role of the proponents of a progressive order is played by the so-called Chicago school of economic liberalism. The experiment conducted by them destroyed the economy and impoverished Russia. In the last few years, we have had a continuous decrease in industrial output, mostly in the light and food industries, in residential construction, and in agriculture. While oil and coal production, fell by a factor of three to four times, with respect to 1989 (which is more than the fall of industry in the first year of W.W.II), the consumer sector was even more debilitated: we produced 60% less textiles, 58% less shoes, 50% less milk products, and so on. This means that our economic crisis has brought the country to a state beyond which lies pure chaos.

However, certain circles of the intelligentsia again prefer not to notice these realities, and label the disenchanted as "red/brown" sympathizers. The situation is even more complicated by the fact that, according to V.A. Perlamutrov, Doctor of Economic Science, we lack a theory which might serve as a beacon for the reformation of the economy and society. Such a theory, in fact, does not exist anywhere in the world. Would this society be able to persevere through the cataclysms of the reforms? Because, according to the basic principles of sociological history, stable and timely development is possible only in a climate of non-antagonistic relations.

In addition to the problems analyzed above in the establishment of enterprise, and its connection to the dynamic social activities of different layers of the population, the question of the preservation of Russia's unity, and reconstruction at the state level stands in tragic poignancy. As the Bolsheviks before them, who, in 1917, placed the interests of world socialism above the interests of Russian statehood, a certain part of the intelligentsia, and the ruling elite love democracy more than Russia, and forget that, should the Russian state collapse, there would be no place for democracy in the geopolitical environment of a Eurasian continent torn by nationalistic hatred.

The latest events in Chechnya serve as a disturbing testament. Questions of state-reconstruction, therefore, are very closely interrelated with problems of national character. The survivability of democracy, its openness and tolerance express themselves in the integration of national values. A number of representatives of the ruling elite inherit the tradition of Marxist thinking, believing that the solution to national interests comes automatically as economic problems are solved. Adherents of other views in the ruling structure, espouse social utopian theories, naively believing that, with the establishment of a New World Order, the eradication of confrontation between countries of differing political orientations, questions of the defense of state interests, and the security of borders and the army will be resolved on their own.

Modern democracy should have a national character, concurrently accepting the pluralism of world cultures. While viewing Russia from a geopolitical vantage point in interaction with other countries of the world, the unique nature of Russia must not be forgotten. Russia is a country which lies on the border between east and west, and, because of this, according to A.S. Panarin, is "doomed to choosing from different civilizations", with a resultant risk of socio-historic instability. Russia is suspended between two centers of gravity, which periodically creates a precondition for the fragmentation of her geopolitical space. Being a link between civilizations, Russia experiences an omnipresent need for a powerful mechanism of integration in the forms of ideology, imperial thinking, and the like. This is another key towards understanding Russia's fate.

So, which are the possible ways for the further development of events? Historic experience of the past indicates that, when society does not know how to react in a situation, it delegates the right to make decisions to the state. The state institutes stern control, and results are achieved by full obedience of the populace to the state, accompanied by consequent great sacrifice.

Social scientists say that this possibility is not out-of-the-question for us.

The case of a society having definite goals, and a clear plan for intense development, is an ideal case, not applicable to the Russia of today. Finally, there is the case when society knows what is to be done, but does not know how to achieve that end. Social scientists hope that it is indeed this third scenario, and not the first, which characterizes today's society.

It is well-known that the backbone of democracy is the middle class – the class of laborers/professionals who own property, according to their abilities and labor, which embodies the foundation of their independence from the state.

When the middle class comprises greater than fifty percent of the population, a society is on the path towards democracy and development.

Each particular moment of historical development determines the future. Today our future depends on the results of the distribution of common resources: either a middle class will be created, which will stabilize the society, or resources will become concentrated in the hands of the few, which, in turn, will be followed by the dictatorship of the minority (in order to maintain their power), or a "black redistribution", i.e. civil war. The latter has not yet occurred, and hopefully never will.

The well of forces, in Russia, which can find a way out of this crisis, has not yet run dry. Despite the fact that the state of crisis has been prolonged, there is an active process of the formulation of alternatives within the society. The great potential of the Russian province, home to the people's initiative, has not been fully utilized. The guarantor of success can only be a strong, constitutional Russian state.

Fyodor Dostoyevsky

Bandakov, Pavel

NOTES OF THE SHIP'S GHOST OR "I HAPPENED TO BE BORN ONCE... "

Foreword

I happened to be born once upon a time on a vast floating object. In the beginning, I did not understand where I was. All around me people said, "Such a thing exists nowhere else, we have the best... " These words provoked me to ask, "What does 'nowhere else' mean, is there something else that exists besides our ship?" But most of the people just sighed and mumbled to themselves... Time passed and everything was awfully gray and usual, but . . . suddenly something happened. That 'something' was supposed to have great consequences, but I noticed none. It was just that the people around me changed, started to bustle, scream, rejoice, cry; in other words, the grayness was replaced by an exuberance. That is when, totally lost, I happened to wander into a faraway corner of the ship, where I usually used to daydream or spent time in contemplation. That day, however, upon entering the room I saw a strange creature sitting in my place at the window, mumbling to itself. Seeing me, the creature started and tried to escape, but then gave up the idea and sat back down. The appearance of the creature interested me and I moved closer. We started talking, but the creature was slow to pick up conversation at first, continually complaining that time these days was moving much faster than before and that it was afraid of something... But then the creature looked up at me with its strange eyes (in one of which there was an obvious sadness, while the other held a strange sparkle) and said, "I know what is bothering you, sit down... "

Chapter 1: Yesterday

"... There was a day when Fair Youth accepted the mission of greatness. Skillful were the hands of these masters, but many years passed before the great labor was finished... ...Then came the day when the ship was lowered into the water; it was great and beautiful in its Byzantine style. The masters went off on a long and dangerous journey. But there was no leader amongst them who knew the art of seafaring and their unity began to disappear...

They landed on a rocky island, where a strong and stern people lived and the masters called upon these people to see if they could find the needed man amongst them. A few good men came forward and accepted the ship and its mission... [1]

Again the brave travelers set off on their journey and their numbers grew. They passed through many islands and cities, and met with dark clouds, which tried to stop and drown the masters. But they overcame these trials and their character was tempered,... and the Great Spirit of the ship was glad.

---

[1] Viking dynasty of Rurik

Then, however, there was great trouble and starvation set in; death was everywhere and merciless fights broke out amongst the masters. The ship's wood cracked and sprung leaks and control over its course was lost, as was its captain.[1]...and this great creation ran aground and, at low tide, the ship capsized on the silted shore among dead seaweed and empty shells; the Great Spirit was sad and many people wandered off. Then, the defenseless ship was attacked by hoards of natives and roaming bandits.[2] And for a long time they robbed the masters who remained with the ship. This oppressed the will of many of the masters and they were beset by grief. However, two great men were among them, Minin and Pozharsky[3]; they uplifted the remaining people and, again, the great and righteous mission was begun; the ship was rebuilt and a new captain elected...

The journey continued on and the ship began to grow. Many islands were visited but the ship soon grew so large it became difficult to steer. The captain (it was Peter)[4] said, "If we want to live, we must modernize the ship." He gathered the people together and gave the orders to begin. The new snow-white sails were raised on the oaken masts, the cannons glittered in the sun. The ship became even greater and they sailed onward, proud of its power, showing itself in foreign ports. There was a great battle near one port with another huge vessel, but our ship stood firm and won its glory.[5]...The ship was growing

---

[1] refers to fragmentation into Russian principalities
[2] refers to Mongol raids
[3] Leaders of popular militia
[4] Peter I oriented Russian development along European lines, and Russia grew into a world power.
[5] War of 1812

and becoming stronger, modernizing on the top decks, but aging down below. Then I went down to the Great Spirit of the ship and it told me: "Yes, you have understood well, it seems that the worst is about to come and even I am unable to get people to listen to reason. Our leaders see what is happening ahead of them, but forget that which lies behind them."

"... But here is our salvation", said the Great One, showing me a book. "Here it is: this book, this art. Our masters are very skillful, and while they are respected among the people, nothing will happen to their creation."...I listened to the Great One with attention, but there in his eyes I saw a fire which I failed to understand...

Years passed and a new captain decided to renovate the ship again from top to bottom. An iron ship was built now, which looked much more powerful and sturdier than those previous...

It went into the waters and continued the voyage, but all was not well on the ship; I saw the Great One again, and saw his concern...

A few short years passed and, in some narrows, a few great ships came into conflict. They were unable to pass one another and there was a horrible battle,[1] with much fire and blood. While the sailors were fighting, one gentleman[2] came down from the top deck to the engine room and told the stokers: "You are working people. All your lives, you live cooped up and in filth. Follow me, I know the way. We will go up to the top decks and you will live in the first class cabins." The working people listened to him and followed up the empty stairs and cor-

---

[1] WW I
[2] P.J. Lenin begins Bolshevik revolution,

ridors, stepping over the dead bodies of the sailors who had fought in the Great Battle. They arrived at the top and the gentleman took the best cabin for himself, while the stokers, marveling at the top decks, were sent back below. The gentleman became captain, locked the course in one direction and overhauled the engine. Seeing the blood and horror, I went down to see the Great Spirit again, but his mood was dark and he would not talk to me; he turned away and left.

The battle ended, the fires burnt out, but the ship was dark and its old doors were locked. Then came the epoch of great grayness. There was a single flash in the fog: two ships collided and a deadly battle began.[1] However sinful our people were, God and the Great Spirit, though unseen, stood by them – I felt that. When I went down to see the Great One after the battle, the passage to him was blocked off. I was scared and it seemed to me that the Great Spirit would never return...

With its locked helm, the ship drifted in ever-decreasing circles, growing decrepit, despite the loud slogans of the captains. Finally the circles became so small, and the ship so disabled, that it came to a standstill.[2] Then a new captain appeared who walked through and opened all the doors of the ship, showing its state to all; and he called for justice, but his voice was weak.[3] Many of the freed people jumped into dingys and rowed into the unknown, while still others drowned. Almost nobody stayed to help the ship.

---

[1] WW II
[2] refers to "zastoy" (stagnation) under Brezhnev
[3] Gorbachev, Perestroika

One day the engines stalled; the shipped drifted by its own inertia and the current. Water gushed in through numerous holes in the hold; fires started which nobody wanted to put out, and those who tried, failed.[1] Every cell of the ship's body moaned; and one even declared that the space between the tenth and the eleventh ribs of the ship was his; he was going to take it over and journey on alone. The ship ran aground again at low tide, as had happened before many years ago...

In despair I went down to look for the Great Spirit again and... saw that the path was open. The Great Spirit of the ship had returned, which means that there is still hope. He had returned at the most trying moment. He looked at me decisively and said: "We must come together, unite, only in that way can we overcome any hardships; ... as our journey, in any case, goes through them. We must work, and we will overcome." So spoke the Great Spirit. I went out onto the deck and called upon the people, but they just waved me off and only two young men said "we must". But with such a small force we were unable to do anything, and now I am in despair. I know not what to do: I am afraid to anger the Great Spirit, I am afraid of myself. If you understand me, take the challenge: unite with the descendants of the first masters/creators, find good people who are not afraid of hard, dirty work. Rebuild this ship. The Great Spirit will always be with you, and now go... go and try... "

---

[1] Breakup of Soviet Union

Chapter 2: Today

And so ended the speech of this strange ghost, which made such a great impression on me.

I emerged from the cabin and walked along the deck, taking note of what was going on there. Suddenly I saw a group of healthy people working diligently at fixing the side of the ship. Some of them were submerged in the ice-cold water, working there... And I understood that my place was among them, among those who were to rebuild the ship anew, which will again embark on a great journey.

P.S. All of Russian history is a ship moving through the oceans of life and time. These oceans have strong currents and stormy winds. Whether or not our ship will prevail, depends on us. My only desire and goal is: to be happy in a happy Russia. So, grant me God, that the majority of our generation should have the goal of seeing Russia happy, of dedicating our lives to her. We trust Russia will be resurrected!

Egor Vereshagin

THE SECOND RENAISSANCE

To tell the truth, the theme of this essay was somewhat un-expected for me, although I had thought about it on occasion. I will try to avoid writing that which has been repeatedly stated in the media. And if you are looking, here, for the news briefs on events of the past and present, and their prognoses for the future, it would be better to turn on the radio. I wish to write an essay which will contain an expression of my private thoughts and feelings, called to life by the theme of this essay, which will be presented here, of course, with facts. I must say that my writing on social and political affairs has always been a weak point. And I can explain why: when I write, I always try to express my deepest, dearest thoughts, penetrating into myself. However, I cannot always substantiate and strengthen these thoughts with facts, and sometimes I fail altogether. This leads me to have to make a choice: to express mostly facts, adding a few opinions to them, or to write what I really think, substantiating these thoughts with a few arguments. I do not know about you, but I prefer the latter. I.S. Turgenev did write, in one of his three famous novels, that the truth belongs to facts. But do not throw my composition in the garbage can immediately! I promise that it will contain some facts.

Even more than assertions, questions will sound here, questions which came to me in multitudes. The first question is the question of time. One can always write something new about Russia, but how should I interpret the words "Yesterday, Today, and Tomorrow"? You see, I could write two pages on how the snow of today has not melted, two pages on how yesterday's season was winter, and an additional three pages on tomorrow's season. To avoid this, I had better write only on that which really touches me... about Russia in the time dimensions known to all of us. To write about today presents the greatest difficulty. It is like a point in geometry: one knows that it exists, and that space is made of its multitudes, but try to catch one of these points for inspection! The present is the not-yet-occurred future, as well as the past-to-be... But, be that as it may, I will still write about the present times in which I live, though they remain undefined. I would be unable to write about time as a whole, especially with regard to a country such as Russia. Further, uniform time does not exist. The great writer Jorge Luis Borges once asked his students: "After Newton, how can we say that only one 'time' exists?" I agree with him. Time is not a singular entity. And what could an eternal, uniform time mean for Russia? To her, time means gigantic ups and downs, as well as chaotic animation and stagnation (zastoy). Unfortunately, stagnation has been much more common. In general, our country is very contradictory. For example, when "zastoy" is mentioned, we think of recent years, during which human rights were encroached upon. Under a dictatorship and an almost totalitarian system of authority. But remember how many kopecks the dollar was worth! Let us wait to pass

50

judgment on the past. The terms our descendants will use to describe the lives of their ancestors will make zastoy seem more like "innocent mischief" – and I am not talking about how much the ruble is worth today and how much it will be worth tomorrow. It is culture, rather our Russian culture – that tears apart my soul. You need facts? If you please! Once, when I became interested in the collected works of Goethe (it matters not that he was German), my mother approached one of the many street-booksellers (whose books can be read by cursory glances at their covers) and asked if he had any Goethe. I was overcome with bitter laughter... But this is no awful history of horrors of the distant future – this is reality! What is most horrific is that, next to these so-called "books", actual classics of S. Esenin, M. Bulgakov, and many others are displayed – Goethe is not present only because he has fallen out of fashion; and fashionable, now, are only those writers who came out against the revolution. Very soon, however, this present, by the laws of time, will turn into the past, and Russian booksellers, when posed the same question, will answer "Who is Goethe?"...

This is truly zastoy. However, I have been distracted with foreign literature and the culture of the past. Our presently living Russian writers and poets, who might be Pushkins or Dostoevskys, who continue to carry the banner of the "Great Russian Culture" (and I have no doubt that it is still alive), are being pushed out by "foreign culture", in such a way that cannot be told with the writer's pen, or in a story in which good triumphs over evil. This is not only happening in literature, but in cinema and music as well.

51

O Great Russian Impasse! How many talents have you ruined? How many loving people have stumbled over you? This impasse is created not so much by the government as by the masses. Overwhelming masses of typical people, who crush those without whom Russia would not exist – the creators. Not so long ago, V. Vysotsky wrote (actually sang):

"Even if you circle the planet,
  without touching it with feet,
  If not one, then another, will fall.
  (bare ice on the land, bare ice!)
  And they'll stomp him to death with boots."

Yes, in our country each must cut his own path. And while Russian lands are rich with gold nuggets, many upstanding people have ended their lives in prisons and jails, and were not only unaccepted, but even unrecognized by their contemporaries. We still have the richest cultural heritage in the world, even though we rarely turn to it in these times. I cannot remember who, but someone said that this was the fate of Russian talent: it does not die, it is beaten, stomped and life is interrupted. For example, Pushkin was killed in a duel, as was Lermontov, Belinsky ended his life in awful poverty, and so on, and so on. There was always something thwarting them: the domination of foreign culture, reactionaries, and censorship. But the harder they were beaten, the greater was their resistance. Remember Lermontov who, until the end of his life, was put down and suffered not because of his extraction, but due to the fact that he was not German. And this is exactly why he not only suffered, but resisted, using all of his talent. Remember as well, Levsha[1] (literary hero of Leskov's writing) and his image as created by the author. His destiny is the tragic destiny of all extraordinary people in Russia.

And independent of the times, what was, is, and will be. There always has been, there are, and always will be uncorrupted people in Russia. While they exist, a Russian soul will always live within us. The impasse does not only mean dead-ends, rather a maze of roads. In this maze everyone seeks their own path. Sometimes they cross, but each has his very own. It is too bad that now, as never before, all Russians are following one heavily-trodden road, and entice others who try to resist. The individual path is too difficult, especially in Russia.

Every Russian poet looking for truth in life and for his place in this world has suffered deprivations and lacked the support of even his closest friends with whom conflicts could not be avoided. But this moral struggle especially arises in the soul of the poet himself. This struggle has, indeed, given rise to great, immortal creations. Remember the separation of the split personality of Gleb Ivanovich Uspensky, the struggle between the revolutionary and the moral-religious in the works of Sergey Esenin, and the conflict between Poet and Citizen, if such had ever taken place at all. I think that often the Poet and Citizen have united in struggle against the Human: poets glorified violence and wars, which citizens created, or, in the best case scenario, remained passive. At the same time, humanist writers and

---

[1] Levsha, a symbolic literary hero, is a uneducated craftsman who outmasters German engineers and whose talents were ignored

citizens of integrity lived in Russia. Even the poets who glorified violence in a name of a cause, showed the negative sides of upheaval. For example, in one of A. Blok's most revolutionary poems, "Twelve", we hear of the violation of the Holy.

Yes, Russia is the most contradictory country. Together with the deep empathy and mercifulness of the Russian character, there also exists unimaginable poshlost (vulgarity) and cruelty – strength goes with weakness. These contradictions have always been the basest elements of Russia, even though the form of the expression of these contradictions constantly changes. For example, today is the great Orthodox holiday – the Epiphany. I was riding on the bus and suddenly heard a babushka (Russian old lady) singing. With clear and resonant voice she sang the prayer. She sang without extending her hand to beg, she sang directly from her soul. It filled the bus! Occasionally she would interrupt the song and say: "Congratulations on the Epiphany!" She quoted the Bible and resumed her singing. Usually, whenever I ride the bus (six times a week), I see tired, angry faces and hear swearing. But that day, there was a serenity which would probably only occur in a church. And here I felt that the atmosphere of tiredness and anger, which usually exists in the commute, had disappeared. Suddenly out side of the bus-temple, there was a traffic jam. The voice of the Babushka skipped, but in a moment, her clear singing continued undistracted.

This means that our culture is not yet dead. The question is... for how much longer? Tomorrow this same babushka will die and one more child will learn the whole lot of Russian curses. But there still are inheritors and carriers of the torch of our culture, which has no analogy in the world. The same child, upon learning these unprintable words will have to make a choice between one and the other and it is on this choice that the destiny of the country depends. I think that our culture will still be reborn. I have even made-up a name for this era – "the Second Renaissance". No, think about it... listen to the beauty in these words... "the second renaissance"! These words will sound literally all over the world, not in Italian, but in Russian – "Vtorore Vozrozhdenie". Yes, indeed there is a rebirth of spirituality in Russia connected with the Russian Orthodox Church, as well as a renaissance of culture: Russian art, with all its strength, will come alive and will be directed towards the re-birth of the inner world of man. Remember Dostoevsky who saw the beginning of this epoch in the Russian faith and church, in the spirituality of the Russian people, and therefore, of the culture as well, since they are all so closely interrelated. If a person has no faith, he will always say and write something wrong... Actually, read Dostoevsky and you will understand my point!

Only prophets and insane people can see the future. I consider myself to be neither of these and will show you a different view. Culture will become business and soul will become body. The machines created by man will enslave him. They will write a new program and computers will slowly replace poets and musicians. The need for culture and morality will disappear. Russia will cease to exist because she cannot live without people dedicated to art and culture – without the righteous ones. Nature will cease to exist, within us and outside of us. Man will be stripped bare, left with only his greed, reason, and cruelty. This may only seem to be a fantastic story, with elements of horror, and perhaps I exaggerated, but all of this is already coming to pass! Of course, I believe more in the first scenario, but do not rule out the second. The future depends on the structure of society, which, in turn, depends on authority, which is precisely that which has posed such major problems for centuries. I am not speaking only of the present. It is a constant problem which faces Russia, with few exceptions. In fact, at the end of the 19th century V. Gilyarovsky wrote:

"Russia has two curses:
Below is the power of darkness,
Above is the darkness of power."

Once, during English class we touched on the question of the rulers of the United States. It turned out that their hero is George Washington. He has become the symbol of America, practically attaining sainthood. Then the teacher asked if we have a Russian equivalent. Here, of course, the name of Peter I was mentioned. I vehemently disagreed. Peter the Great? Is he not the same man who, having axed the window to Europe, used the same axe to cut down Russian traditional roots and destroy the sources of Orthodox culture? Yes, he concurrently developed science, strengthened Russian power and brought about major change... built Petersburg... but Petersburg, as his other achievements, was built on human bones. So, is there no ideal hero in our history, who might be portrayed on our ruble notes? I searched extensively, especially for this composition, but still have not found such a figure. Even though many have tried to improve the state of their country, their results were always detrimental. Some thought of the people as "masses", some of Russia as "land", forgetting the people entirely.

The majority of the rulers did not think at all. I think that, in significance and with regard to the size of the deeds for the good of Russia, Ivan the Terrible comes right after Peter the Great. And if anything, Ivan was "terrible", and hardly an ideal ruler. I will not explain why. (See Chronology, ed.) By the way, it is indeed Ivan who built the first plumbing in the palace from which they scooped and drank water. While the lead, from which the pipes were made, had a negative effect on the brain...

There never was, not ever in Russia, a just power. And still there is not. From the point of view of social science, in a state where ruling circles are responsive to only a slight degree, to the opinions of the people, authoritarian regime clearly establishes itself. Also, almost all types of power are concentrated in one well-known individual. I do not speak of the events which have been started by ours and the Chechen government. If the Russian language possessed the words to describe that venture, and all of those events in which and in whose name blood is being spilled, I would have written about that as well.

Therefore... authoritarianism. We cannot yet even consider democracy. The most important aspect of democracy is the communication of conscious people and reasonable government, and that is exactly what we are lacking. First of all, there is a need to view people, not as a mass, but through the expression of each individual of the people. Only then will people become conscious. Indeed, with the development of individual personality, a rebirth of the soul and culture takes place. This is

57

why the future is ours... No, not ours, but **mine**! Even though I now feel that the possibility of a transition to totalitarianism is very likely. Who would not want to see the appearance of some tyrant, cruel, just, of strong will power, who would kick out the present pathetic government? But, truly and actually, such a ruler would repair the economy and restore Russian international stature, and put down that part of the culture, which he dislikes, and which, according to the third law of Newton, would be reborn enriched and developed. After that, other forms of culture would be reborn, the economy improved, as well as science, and finally there would be an appearance of human consciousness among Russian citizens, as their spirituality grew. The dictatorship would slowly be replaced by a democracy brought into being by culturally enriched Russians. This will mark the beginning of the epoch of the Second Renaissance. However, another way is possible: if the present zastoy continues for another twenty years, people's consciousness will fall so low that they will truly turn into automatons in a thoughtless mob. Culture will become business since the only thing which can destroy culture is inaction. The soul will become body. The machines will enslave humanity. Actually, I already said that.

I cannot imagine the transition from our present state to democracy. It is also difficult to imagine how democracy will ever exist in Russia. Such is the contradictory nature of our country.

I now come to the point at which that phrase so loved by all is usually pronounced. When our government commits mistakes this phrase is immediately utilized. This is approximately how it happens: Some reporter, after broadcasting that our country, while having plentiful fields, buys grain from America, snidely and thoughtfully adds: "Well, it's not for nothing that it is said that 'Russia cannot be comprehended by mind alone... '" Gentlemen! Don't you think that the great Russian poet, (trust me, he was no foreigner) wrote of the same country that you speak of – which can be measured with a common yardstick. O, if only Fyodor Ivanovich Tyutchev could have known what would be made of his poetry, he would never have written it!:

"By mind alone – not to be known,
By common yardstick – not to be gauged:
She has her own stately stature
In Russia one must only trust."

This Tyutchev wrote, having had faith in, and having tried to understand Russia all his life, and saw that she was too infinite for small, evil human minds. Those who speak these words spitefully, do not understand Russia at all, because they do not understand the world with their minds, but by other parts of their bodies, which are probably very well-developed.

No, my homeland is not the government, not social and economic structures. First of all, it is unusual people. The saints... and while we have such people Russia will live and flourish. These people still exist here. Whoever they may be: poets, who may not even write poems, painters, musicians, writers, politicians, regular folk, indeed without three of these (as according to the Russian proverb), without three saints, a Russian city cannot stand. It is from their action that the soul enlivens and cleanses itself and the mind sobers. Of course, all of this could not come from anywhere else, but from our great mother, without whom all would suffocate and die, which is Russian nature. These two entities are inseparable, they cannot exist without each other. Indeed, it is nature which has always given us its beauty and power, both physical and spiritual.

A great power and wisdom emanates from every blade of grass, from every gulp of cold spring water, from every breath of fresh woods and fields in the wind. Miracle, our extraordinary miracle! And that very miracle we do not understand and value: we are ready to stomp out any flower and pollute the rivers and poison the air. The same goddamn rivers of which the poet wrote: "... oceans of her flooding rivers... " It is not a human, but indeed nature which is the symbol of our country. This is where the whole of Russia's essence lies. Understand the meaning of a simple forest flower, and you will understand your homeland. Understand a simple birch! Actually, she is not so simple. She is the embodiment of all Russian beauty and is her symbol. When you are in the birch woods... oh, sweet moments! Your wounded soul is cured. One is calm as never before, and at the same time drunk, the heart pounds harder. One is filled with the unusual fresh energy of the birch woods. And how many material gifts the birch has given us!... And we gave it its due accordingly. Actually, the beauty of the birch has not only been contemplated by Russians alone. Our literature teacher once told that this tree only grew here in Russia. It is true in the meaning that it is a Russian symbol, that it was never as esteemed as here. But remember the following lines:

"Give me bark, O birch tree,
Give your yellow bark, O birch tree,
You, standing in the valley,
With beautiful stature above the small trees."

This is the due given by other peoples, even though Bunin, translating this poem, undoubtedly thought of our Russian birch tree (but between ours' and others' birch trees, there is a big difference). We also give her her due by the names which are preserved until our day. If one opens an encyclopedic dictionary, one will find curious facts: Berezina is a river in western Russia, a tributary of the Dnepr, Bereyoza in the Brest region, Berezino is a city in the Minsk region, Berezniki is a city in the Perm region, and so on.

What is the current situation? Except for the names on the kiosk, "Beriezka", and the conservation of the birch as a type of tree, we do not thank her. This is the way we pay our dues to nature to which all the representatives of Russian culture have bowed over the centuries. How then, are we to understand Russia... ? This resource is a great miracle, and we must do something with it! At least not what we are doing now... "Stop and look. Enjoy the beauty. To contemplate. To stop, not for twenty minutes,... no, stopping for beauty one forgets time... stop for two hours. Only then will the beauty engage you, only then is a deep spiritual contact possible, and hence the experience of joy." V. Solouhin. Indeed it is such a unity of the Russian people and Russian nature, which existed for so many years, that has given birth to the great works of art. Is it really

61

impossible to do this now? The destiny of Russia depends on this contemplation of miracles!

Actually, I, myself, do not get that many chances to unite with nature. Only for a few days over the holidays do I go to the village to hunt. I have to say, our village is very unusual; it used to be owned by a remarkable Russian landowner, Alexander Nikolaievich Karamzin. Not the famous writer, but a relative. This landowner did a lot to improve the lives of his peasants, but was no stranger to aesthetics either. He conceived of a project for a beautiful park and completed it. But since then the park has been abandoned. It is neglected and overgrown, even though one can still see its beauty. The wonderful man-made ponds are stagnating, and the fish have almost died out. Karamzin also built a hospital for the peasants. It is still in its original state, even though it now serves people from the entire region. The memory of this man is held in esteem. They have erected a cross for him in the most beautiful part of the park.

What great hunting grounds this estate had. During my father's youth there was an over-abundance of black grouse. Later, the wily Soviet government decided to spray the village fields with pesticides, where the black grouse young seek refuge. It was the end of the species in the region. Hazel grouse and wood grouse diminished in number as well. However, in the fall of this year I saw my first wood grouse. And while we were walking in the fields, from afar I saw a flying black grouse. God-willing, the grouse will come back.

What is most important is not to scare them! You hear? Do not scare and poison them in vain! Better yet, take a rifle (I am not kidding) and, enjoying the fresh air, walk into the depths of the woods; not necessarily to kill something, but to merge with nature. Only then will the beauty engage your spirit. And this is possible only here in Russia! Something must be done with this great Russian miracle. How can the Russian person become active in this relation? Especially since spring is on its way – the time of enlivening, of waking up from dreams. Meanwhile the snow has not yet melted. And it will be winter tomorrow in Russia...

Peter the Great

Glushaeva, Svetlana

THE RUSSIAN INTELLIGENTSIA

"Chances flew close by, like bullets,
Stray bullets, delayed, blind at the end of their flight.
Some of us risked standing up,
And some caught glory, some bit the dust.

.   .   .

We will put candles at the heads of the dead,
Those who had died from unimaginable love."

V. Vysotsky

I consider it both possible and necessary to write on this particular theme, within the context of "Russia: Yesterday, Today, Tomorrow", since I am strongly convinced that the destinies of both the intelligentsia and Russia are so intertwined that it is impossible to consider them separately. The destiny of Russia is the destiny of the intelligentsia.

In conversations on Russia one always comes across words like intelligentsia, intelligent, and intelligentnost. While these ideas are both pertinent and fashionable today, the true meaning of this phenomenon, unfortunately, has been slowly disappearing. What is left is just a myth. (It is not without reason that this term is not used to describe people, rather their ap-

64

pearances, for example: "he has an intelligent beard".)
Furthermore, we often mix up the two different ideas of intelligentny and intellectual. Very often, people who are well-read are associated in our minds with "intelligentny". It is a sad fact that five of ten upper-classmen, at a minimum, and many adults will (without a doubt) make this mistake. Incidentally, this phenomenon is part of our culture: the notions of Russia and the intelligentsia have been, and will always be inseparable. This is uniquely Russian, ours, native; in the West, which is so progressive and advanced, even somewhat cynical, and which seeks to define everything and place it within a narrow context of qualification, such a word simply does not exist. There is a close English word "intelligent". But it only means "developed, smart, talented, quick-witted", and is no equivalent for "intelligentsia".

So, what does this idea mean? Let us turn to history. At mid-century, the Russian writer Boborikin gave the following definition: "the person of intellectual labour, the person who contributes to the creation of spiritual values, and one who selflessly serves a noble idea". Therefore, two fundamentals can be reduced: the synthesis of spiritual values and idealism. But, knowing Russia, we can add a third: being in opposition to government, to authority...

Poor, long-suffering Russia!... she was never lucky with her rulers. History seems to always place short-sighted, illiterate individuals, or bloodthirsty tyrants at the helm of the great ship of Russia. Being short-sighted, they have set the course towards miraculous goals. A bitter fate awaited those who dared to elevate themselves higher than the prescribed lim-

65

its, who tried to have Russia avert the crash, and avoid the reefs and rocky shores.

The intelligentsia's history begins much earlier... but allow me to start my chronicle in the 18th century, since "... in reality, this wide social movement is born with Peter, is his child, who has legitimately inherited his legacy."

First of all, I want to talk about M.V. Lomonosov. He thought about global problems which remain urgent to this day:

– the growth and preservation of the Russian people;

– the improvement of disposition, and education among the folk...

Are these not the same questions which are being tackled by the Russian intelligentsia? His ideas, however, remained neglected. They were forgotten, as all that is good and important is forgotten here in Russia. Do not be surprised by the jump in time, but we are already in the 19th century. Let us talk of its heroes as well. Pestel, Muravyov-Apostol, and Trubetskoy... these people were advanced, smart, educated men, who understood the impending crash of the system in which they existed, and who, without a doubt, loved Russia and the Russian people, and took their fateful steps, not in self-interest, but for the good of the Fatherland. Yes, destiny showed them no mercy, it threw them into the catacombs, but they moved Russia, once again fired the spark, which almost went aflame in the patriotic war of 1812, but then was accurately stomped out by the careful Emperor. But,

"Your doleful labor will not be wasted,

And the high aspirations and strivings of your minds will not be lost... "

Such was the prediction of Pushkin, and his prophecy held true.

It was indeed the Decembrists who prepared the soil for the liberals, who represented the merger of "the sobriety of political realism with clear determination to withstand popular opinion." Understanding all of the difficulties of Russia's current state of affairs, they wanted changes, even if they came from above, and even if they were   gradual. It is indeed because of the liberals that Russia cast off the yoke of serfdom, which had been a burden for centuries. This was a first major victory of the Russian intelligentsia, and probably the last.

The liberals have faded into the background, after serving their purpose. In their place, in the uncertain, unbalanced times of transition, when that which originally constituted the foundation of Russia, faith in the Czar and God, was being lost, came the Revolutionaries. They were honest, strong, fearless and brave, they were destroying the existing order and, in doing so, were crossing themselves out.   In their world view, a horrific substitution took place: mercy was exchanged for cruelty, and the love of people was exchanged for the idolization of people.   It is no coincidence that, in dreaming of the revolution, they achieved their goal through terror. Their "love of people" was not the same as loving one's neighbor, which Dostoevsky wonderfully illustrated in his novel "The Possessed", in which a similar sect of revolutionaries, in the name of their high and beautiful ideals, commit murder. Further – "The love of equal justice and common welfare... almost destroyed interest in truth." Their heroes become "hyperbolic Rahmetovs", who know no fear, no pain, no love, who are possessed by "the great idea." These kinds of people were needed to stand at the helm, at the opportune moment, to lead the crowds to the high and wonderful goal. This is what they thought and they were mistaken. The mob cannot tell good from evil, that criterion which belongs to all of us loses itself in the mob. And what if the mob is lead by calculating fanatics?

But, finally, that, of which many generations of intelligentsia had dreamt, came to pass. Inequality was liquidated, peasants received land, and Russia was declared a republic with all the attendant attributes: freedoms of speech, press, and faith. But the picture quickly changed, and returned to its prior state, in that the exploiters and exploited simply switched positions; the absolute monarchy was replaced by a dictatorship of the bureaucratic elite, under the guise of the dictatorship of the proletariat.

It seemed that no one noticed this substitution (podmena), the intoxication of the revolution was too strong. Only part of the intelligentsia understood the situation, but they were forced to leave.

> "O mountain of blackness,
> which covered – all the world!
> It's time, it's time, it's time!
> To return the ticket to the Maker.
> I refuse – to be.
> In the bedlam of non-humans,
> I refuse – to live.
> With the wolves of the squares,
> I refuse – to howl.

With the sharks of the plains,
I refuse to swim –
Downstream over the backs of the dead,
I need no holes,
Of ears, no eternal eyes,
To your crazy world,
There is one answer – Refusal."

Marina Tsvetaeva

They left this land. The "ship of philosophy" pulled out of port. Esenin, Mayakovsky, Tsvetaeva, Bulgakov, Gumilev, whose souls were "pure bruise" left us for many years of prohibitions, iron curtain, and walls. But these sacrifices were not enough. In the camps and jails, the talented and freedom-loving youth were killed (remember "Children of Arbat", by Rybakov). The country did not need thinkers, it needed only machines. This is why the famous show-trials of sabotage took place (for example, the trial of the engineers). The best parts of the clergy were being annihilated as well, those who were the carriers of good, beauty, and truth, and, who could truly be called intelligentsia.

But the roots were too deep to be pulled out and destroyed forever. The 1960's raised another generation, which came out against the system. Yes, there were too few of them, they were doomed, and, generally speaking, nothing happened. But to say that their sacrifice was in vain would be sacrilege. Theirs was an attempt to reach people's minds and hearts. And that attempt found a response.

These awful and critical years could not break down the Russian intelligentsia. It grew in strength, it lead, lighting the pitch darkness: Solzhenitsin, Tendryakov, Sakharov, Brodsky, Vysotsky, Lihachyov, and thousands of others who are little known to us.

The years passed... All that our people went through now seems like a bad dream, but today – it is the same horror, the same black and impenetrable darkness. We are bogged down in the details of everyday life, petrified, indifferent, ... truly, we are the same frightened people and the following principle still rules: "My house is on the outskirts (I will not get involved)". We are still not ready for the powerful protest. We still are faced with a choice between the spiritual and moral, and the material, because these are so irreconcilable. Despite all of this, there are still people who light small sparks in the souls of those around them. I speak first and foremost of the teachers: they have always been, and will always be on the frontline. The development of the generation of the 80's and 90's depends on these teachers. It is as if they are passing the baton in a relay.

We have a difficult journey ahead of us. It is because (if one recalls the past) the history of the Russian intelligentsia is either "martyrdom, or the registers of Russian jails". The Russian way is a path of forgeries and cheating, because, even now in my view, there is a counterfeiting of values taking place: democracy is substituted by agitators, the freedom to which we all aspired turned into anarchy and bespredel (actions unbounded by any moral code)...

But a lot depends on us. I will not write bad of my generation, since a lot has already been written, and since it is not true of all of us. It seems to me that we can bravely accept the baton, since that which makes up the idea of intelligentsia is made up of small characteristics and nuances, which our generation has not yet lost:

- the ability to understand others

- readiness to help

- tolerance towards the world and people

- hospitality and civility

- respect for cultural traditions

- responsibility in resolving moral issues

- richness and correctness in one's language

I bow before these people who made the first steps on this thorny path. And thanks is due to those who forged the road for us. I think that our generation will be able to help Russia in the future.

Grigoryeva, Irina

A LETTER FROM THE YOUNG GENERATION

Greetings Dear Sis,

I received your letter yesterday. Many thanks for your congratulations and the latest news. I am glad that all is well with you.

Marina, I was saddened by some parts of your letter. You write that American businessmen want to buy some land on the Klyazma river in order to build a factory. But what will happen to the conservation lands? Why do the local authorities not put a halt to this plan? Why are the people silent? This is our land, our nature! It is hard to imagine that, in place of the virgin woods, there will stand a large smoke-spewing plant, for which the need is unknown.

To tell you the truth, I feel pain when I think of our country. Look around for yourself. We are on our way, not only to a full economic collapse, but headed towards moral degradation as well. On the streets I see embittered, tired-out faces. Doesn't it seem to you that people are slowly turning into beasts?

In everyone's heads, one word echoes like a bell, "vyzhit" ("survival"). To survive by any means. Animal instincts are overpowering the human mind; wanton violence rules. Criminal chronicles multiply with each passing day: the preva-

72

lent notion being to survive at the expense of the weak, even if you have to shed blood. And the weak... ? In the country I hope such things do not exist, but, here, I see beggars, from three to eighty years of age, daily. Children, who should be playing with dolls, approach you and timidly ask for money. And their faces... thin and pale as if only one drop of life remained there! While I reach for money I watch the hopeless sadness and despair give way to happiness and gratitude, a doglike loyalty. ...And the old ladies! Stretching out their hands, hardly able to stay on their feet, they beg: "Give in God's name." You know, Marina, I imagine how they fought on the frontlines fifty years ago, how they stood at the machines in the factories, how they starved in wartime, how they waited for peace and dreamt of how their homeland, raised from ruin, would repay them for their suffering. And the result? What is terrible is that all of this is within the framework of normality. Ten years ago we prided our selves: "We have no unemployment!" And now, even this can no longer be said. Large lay-offs from the workplace give rise to the slogan: "Every man for himself!"

Marina, our times remind me of the 30's, which grandmother recalls with a shudder: the era of economic crisis, Stalinist repression, violence and the oppression of individuality. Russia, then, trod on millions of dead bodies and we were, paradoxically, saved by the war. The decaying politics of Stalin were revealed to all, but what is most important, people began once again to unite under the common goal of the war effort. In speaking of the 40's we remember the heroic deeds of the Soviet people. History repeats itself. I am afraid that today's political structure will soon be interpreted as a dictatorship of oligarchy. Truly, our government makes daily legislation, the traces of which are unfound in real life, (only a steady inflation of prices). And who approved the decision to start the war with Chechnya? For what reason are hundreds of our boys dying there? It is a question asked by millions of people. I believe, and I think you will agree with me, that Yeltsin's policies are criminal. The lines of Lermontov come to mind:

"O how will you pay, Tyrant?
 For this righteous blood,
 For the blood of the people, the blood of citizens.
 When the scales appear
 And the judge weighs them
 Will your hair not stand on end?
 Will your hands not tremble?
 You will turn with pleading eyes
 And the bloody columns proclaim
 The guilty verdict: Guilty, guilty!"

Is this quote not appropriate to those in power right now? It seems to me that only an ancient, subconscious belief in the "Good Czar, the Father" is preventing people from taking action. But how long will this belief last? A year or two, followed by further bloodshed? I love my country; I am not indifferent to its fate. It is sad to see that Russia is gradually loosing its culture, bit by bit, becoming a second USA. Yes, we must maintain friendly and business-like relations with other countries, value their cultures and respect their laws. But do we have to have only foreign goods in our stores, must we prefer the English language over Russian, do we need American cinematic thrillers over good-old Russian comedies? Why is it all leading to the situation of "... no Russian sound and no Russian face around"?

Understand, Marina, I am afraid for the next generation. Might it happen that they should only experience the remains of our national culture in museums? Lermontov writes on this as well:

"I greet you, Holy cradle of the war-like Slavs,
A traveler returned from foreign lands.
Elated, I looked upon the weathered walls
Through which the changes of the centuries
Have passed unharmfully, where the bell on the assembly tower
Tolled in freedom's name, and rang on in its destruction
Taking with it, in its fall, many a proud soul.
Tell me, Novgorod, is it true they are no more?
And is your Volhov (river) not the Volhov of the past?"

Our culture begins with the legacy of ancient Russia, which was rich in its religious and secular forms. This culture carried within itself a myriad of bright expressions of feeling, reflected in legend and song. Our task is not only to preserve the historic memorials of Russia (literature, monasteries, kremlins, national cemeteries), but to expand this collection, and to give our grand-children an enriched legacy.

You know, Marina, I wish I had lived at the time of Peter the Great. I admire the sharp mind, tact, and political flexibility of this man. During his rule, the stature of Russia had been raised to an unprecedented height. Foreign countries found out how powerful Russia could be. It was the era when "... With a sideways glance, other peoples and states step aside and yield the path to her." (Gogol) Peter the Great was the first to look into the root of education and, thanks to his reforms, a great coryphaeus such as Lomonosov could arise. "The Russian always desired the impossible, always, with hungry soul, he lived to strive... This is the origin of his success."

Of course it is unfortunate that not all of the Czars could do as much for the state. But who else sat on the Russian throne!... Ivan the Terrible, famous for the Oprichnina (secret police); the weak-minded Prince Fyodor; the Polish Prince Vladislav; and Boris Godunov, who irrevocably enslaved the peasants. Russia also knew such profligates as Catherine II, and reformers such as Alexander I. It is hard to name them all. This is our history which we must value. There are dirty spots in this history, when a "great sadness of the people overfilled our land": serfdom, militarism, and Stalin's repression. But there are also things to be proud of. It seems to me that there exists no other nation in the world that has suffered and survived through as much as has Russia: one-hundred and seventy years of the Tartar-Mongol yoke did not break down our ancestors, did not stop their aspirations for freedom, and the multiple wars did not embitter the hearts of the peaceful farmers. I agree with Asadov:

"Freedom! O how hot it is!

And how beautiful its echo is,

It was not for nothing that Sten'ka Razin, on the block,

Looked, with a grin, at the executioner!

And was it not for these holy words,

For the truth, clean as the sunrise,

That Pugachev laid down his head,

And for a quarter-century, by the sound of shackles,

The Decembrists dragged out in exile,

And people remember, they are coming...

And there is no stopping them,

And there will be more of them from year to year.

So that you could live and dream in this world without fear,

To think openly and speak

In short, so that there would truly be freedom!"

People do not forget. I am sure that any Russian, with a sense of deep gratuity and admiration, remembers the heroism of the Soviet people during the years of the Great Patriotic War. We cannot forget how, in the freezing weather, those in the rear worked multiple shifts on the machines, tearing the skin off of their hands, ignoring the pain. Many books have been written of these great deeds. I can never hold back the tears when I watch the film "The Dawns Are Quiet Here", where, touchingly and simply, the character of the true Russian man is shown: to give everything for their motherland, to save the children from Hitler's genocide.

I think, Marinka, that you will agree that, when we declare our nationality, we should hold our heads high, with pride.

I have been reading Gogol again lately and found a line ideally suited to our times: "Russia, where are you racing to... ?" Truly, where?

Around me I see my peers wound up by superstars of American entertainment. Around me, I hear street jargon and not the melodious Russian language. In the stairways I see empty bottles and syringes for the well-known goals. This is beastly and amoral.

> "With sadness I look at our generation!
> Its future either empty or dark...
> ... To good and evil, we are shamefully indifferent,
> At the start of undertakings, we wilt without a fight.
> Before danger, we are all faint-hearted,
> Before the power, we are just filthy slaves...
> And we are bored by ancestral traditions...
> As a sullen and soon-to-be-forgotten crowd,
> We will pass through life without sound or trace,
> And our ashes...
> ... Our descendants will insult with scornful poems.'

Yes it is hard to save the spiritual river-bed in a world where cataclysms occur every minute. But it should not be any other way. I often turn to literature and become more convinced each time that history is periodic, it repeats itself. If I were to be asked: "What period of our epoch would you like to replace our times with?" I would answer, none! Russia has always suffered, spilled seas of blood and survived nonetheless.

"... And the eternal strife,
The peace is just in our dreams... "

She will survive these times as well, because the Russian is the legendary hero, Ilya Muromets. He is the boss of the land, he is his own boss. As Edmund Hillary said: "We conquer not the mountains, but ourselves." Russia is now at the crossroads, but she has been there before. Our salvation is to overcome wild behavior, to unite, to elect the smart, educated, and talented "Czar-father", and to rebuild Russia.

I wish that my grandchildren, besides rock and roll, also listened to Bach, Tchaikovsky, and Mozart; that they not only read Terminators I, II, III... , but also the timeless works of Dostoevsky, Gogol, and Pushkin. I wish for laws equating the lives of animals to human life. Otherwise, engineers will have to artificially create rabbits, moose, and squirrels. Coming out onto the street I long to see smiles on the faces of the passers-by. I would like, with full right, to declare "You Russia, are racing as a spry, unpassable troika (three-horse team)".

Is it not true, Marinka, that millions wish for the same thing, but that meanwhile "Russia still looks for trails to lead it back home."

Until I see you again, Sis.

P.S. I know not how you will react to this outpouring of emotions, but I am still interested in your opinions. Please write me.

Gushin, Mikhail

THE RUSSIAN SOUL

The theme presented for this essay is a complex one, one that presents a great challenge, even to college students and professionals. It probably should not have been posed, even at the college level. Whatever form of presentation one chooses in response, demands a 'colossal baggage' of intellectual experience. Even common sense does not suffice in this case; there is a need for wisdom attained through suffering the trials and tribulations of life, which people are thrown into.

Philosophers have argued and historians erred in their explications of the historical path of Russia. They contradict one another in their attempts at solving the mysteries of the great Russian soul and in their explanations of the great Russian spirituality... Wise ones took wrong paths, got lost and could not find their way out. It seems impossible, from the vantage point of the limited life experience of the a young person's mind, and the corresponding limited education, to try to observe the expanse of the destinies of "Rus"...

One can read clever (insightful) books about the past, even try to form one's own opinions. In the past, we might even find processes whose evaluations do not seem contradictory, and which, at least, do not cast doubts into the present (though this is still very rare). At any rate, there is still no realistic possibility to look objectively at "today", when we do not possess the ability to accept events soberly and rationally –, emotions take precedence in our perception of current events... There are tanks in Moscow and we are overwhelmed by fear and horror. Through this prism of horror we submissively believe, and thirstily absorb information which races at us from all sides. First impressions leave their marks on the perceptions of those following. What seems gigantic and meaningful today, might be small and insignificant tomorrow...

To peek into tomorrow seems initially easier than evaluating today's events – since, when trying to make prognoses, we lean on historical trends of the past; (something I have already touched upon). It is very difficult to make predictions. It is a task for great philosophers. One need not be a philosopher to predict the coming of the next price increases. But few are granted the ability to predict greater processes ...

Does this country have a destiny? Is the term "destiny" even appropriate? Does destiny itself exist? What world order assigned this "destiny" – the role countries were born to play.

A very original approach to the problem of national destiny has been presented by L. Gumilev. His theory is insightful, very well structured and, most importantly, mathematically exact. It is reasonable to assume that any civilization usually exists for about 1500 years and, in comparing the charts of pasionarnost[1] intensity of super-ethnic systems, it is easy to see the commonality in the historical development of ethnos...

---

1 Instinctual passion for life

But for all its merits, this theory is very cruel. The time frames are rigid and dry, and the levels of evolution are predetermined. If it is to be considered that Russia is not an exception to the rule, then the picture of our future is a very gloomy one indeed. Slavic ethnos is at the stage of breakage, after which, according to Gumilev's theory, there is no regeneration.

Were the philosophers wrong, then, in thinking that a renaissance of the Great Russia would save the world? Is it possible that Russia might wilt before fulfilling its mission, a mission that would then remain undiscovered? Did philosophers not say that the future belonged to the Slavs, and not to the economically developed modern countries – they did not even mention economics. The fact that we are now stomping ourselves into the dirt; that we are afraid to be Russian, will never allow us to become a great nation! Could this in fact already have occurred? Is Gumilev right, are we the dying mammoths of this age?

Should I make a foolish joke now... but no!... why foolish? Indeed, have we failed to fulfill one great mission while taking on another – left to us from above, so we would not be insulted? For how long now have we been showing the world *how not to live.* We sacrificed ourselves to show to all the mistakes of historical development; so that others would be able to avoid them. Are we to become the new Christ, come to save humanity? Maybe this is the second coming? Russia the great Jesus?... Holy One?...

There are more questions than answers. But perhaps this mission, given in consolation, is the "great mission"?... Even though it is very doubtful that our great sacrifice was a conscious one; that we accepted the burden of the mistakes consciously... But, for now, we humbly carry our cross.

How many times has Russia saved the world? At least twice: two invasions drowned in Russia, two wars – 1812 and the Second World War; though they are not of equal value as will be seen below.

Did the imperial designs of Napoleon carry a threat for humanity? The question is contradictory. Light and happy came the French, they were motivated by unlimited boldness and youthful fervor; the lust for riches. They wanted new land; they wanted to show their strength. The French were able to fight like animals and die like heroes. But they did not have hate for people... they did not... and that is it. The idea of national superiority did not send them into battle, they desired the drunken feeling of victory over one's opponent... It is superfluous to mention how multinational their armies were or how primitive their looting relationship was to the conquered nation. Their proud ambition did not represent a danger to humanity as a whole.

On the other hand, how far the science of destruction went in the twentieth century, the century of progress? Napoleon could not have dreamt of the plans of Hitler. He, indeed, understood that the notion of populating the entire world with French was simply unrealistic. Never could the idea of ethnic superiority have occurred to him. Now, however we have had to deal with the planned and sharply directed annihilation of peoples, large and small. A threat like the threat of fascism in the 20th century had never been seen: anti-human theory implemented on such a large scale. Of course, anti-semitism had existed, Africans had been enslaved, Native Americans put on reservations... But there had never existed such methodology, such a precisely planned program; and Russia overcame that idea and killed it... saved the world!

The Tartar-Mongol invasion? It is possible that its scale has been forever enlarged and exaggerated... by everybody, beginning with the first witness, and ending with the modern historian. Gumilev thoroughly proved that the invasion was done by no more than forty thousand people. Granted, this was a huge and terrifying force in feudal times when the only defenses were local guards and weary militia, not even sure of whom they should fear and fight against in those times of numerous local wars,... but Russia stood strong and even though the Mongols won, they got trapped in the "gigantic spaciousness", they grew tired of weak but stubborn resistance. Knowing how those who made it roamed over regions of Europe, we could guess that, if Russia had not slowed and weakened the "steppe people", the Czechs probably would not have endured, and what might have ensued, in the rest of Europe, lies beyond the limits of our imaginations. Europe was also being torn by feudal divisions – the nascent weakness of any developing statehood...

Many times Russia has stood in front of the invasion as a shield. This nation has always stood as an impenetrable wall. But, who is it that lives here then? Who are these people? What is this mysterious Russian soul?

The same groups still live here. Peoples and their leaders. Intelligentsia, clerks,...

As things stand, the majority of the people are good. One need not explain who the Russian people are to those who know, but one must bring to attention particular characteristic traits.

The people of Russia are phenomenally apolitical. The full anarchy of these people has been carried throughout our history. There is no other such anarchy in any country, as that of Russia (this is one thing we can be proud of). A referendum is held and people do not go to vote: "I am lazy, and what can I really influence?" This Russian national laziness and slowness is a special subject.

Why will we never build a fully democratic, Western-style democracy? Because democracy in itself demands that everybody partake in the political process... Babushkas do not attend referendums and, when they do, they scratch out every name but the last one ("What can I influence anyway?")

Berdyaev already wrote that Russia waits for its leaders like "the red girl waits for her intended one" (as brides wait for the groom) She will never venture out by herself in search of happiness; happiness should come to *her*... but its not there, not there...

Why has Russia always been under foreign domination? Because there never was a hybrid birth of western culture in Russia; the western principals of management have not penetrated Russian soil. Russia stayed virgin pure and therefore could not be governed in new ways. Monarchy, full absolutism was her fancy.

The Slavic race is deeply feminine in its nature. In order to govern Russia in new ways, there was a need for a masculine impulse. A truly masculine race is the Germanic race. For many years – two full centuries Russia was governed, its key positions held, by the descendants of the Germanic peoples. The Romanovs, since the 19th century, had more German blood in them than Russian; the last emperor was not Russian at all...

Because of its exceptional anarchism, Russia likes to give the power away to someone else: "Here, take care of it"... while Russia, herself, continues to sleep. It would seem that in this case the ideal governor would be a quiet, level-headed, peaceful individual. But as we can see from experience, Russia loves strong, cruel governors. And what is more important and paradoxical: she loves... progress!

Nicholas II became "the bloody one", because of the simple greed of people who stampeded for free goods. Peter the Great paved the roads with dead bodies, flooded Russia with the blood of recalcitrance – nobody knows how many died on the first construction sites. But that push which Russia experienced, that rise of the Russian empire, people will never forget, and its blessed legacy will live on for centuries to come. (The same could be applied to Ivan IV, "the terrible", as well as others.)

Is this characteristic not a viable explanation of the Russian love of "father Stalin" and Andropov, who "had things in order"?

There is another love of the Russian people – the genetic love of VOLYA. An analogical concept to VOLYA does not exist anywhere else. It is not possible, even in Russian, to explain this idea. It can only be felt. What is VOLYA? ...sleep on as long as you like, drink by the bottle, take off riding at high speed... ("What Russian does not like a fast ride?" – Gogol) ... to drink into stupor, to fly! To get a monthly stipend and spend it all, not caring that you will suffer for the next month...

Ach! Swing from the shoulder! Let fly my hand! Go wild, soul! ... to the mother anarchy!

In the circumstances of the predisposition to VOLYA, there is a right for the existence, if only for a paragraph, of the universal right to idleness in any place at any time. VOLYA – carousal, the Great Russian Laziness, the Great Russian Spirit, is the most absurd expression of itself. VOLYA – a spiritual upsurge to which scale no other national character is capable. VOLYA – the symbol of Russia.

Do not even think of giving people freedom. FREEDOM is not what people need... they would rather have some kind of dictator (as was usually the case throughout history). Don't think of giving them freedom – freedom of speech, faith, and press. They don't need your democratic ideals... they need VOLYA! If you give the Russian people freedom; say freedom of press... the next day, in that same press, you will be mocked and accused of softness. People are similar to misbehaving first graders and their governors are the idiots of the tenth grade. If the latter speaks as an equal to the people, he will immediately be chased by a screaming, primitive, name-calling crowd...

"Don't let me, O God, see a Russian revolt! Meaningless and merciless... " (Pushkin) There is a scary, dark, wildly primordial Russian essence. The most terrifying force is the mob: the mob armed with their cudgels, going for VOLYA. The mob does not think of what comes afterwards (another characteristic of the great Russian soul)... Self-interested leaders use the mob as a weapon, as a tank, for example. But whatever the leaders say, the crowd always goes after VOLYA; whatever the leaders promise, the mob always moves to its desired goal – VOLYA. It might be a small episode, but at least some windows will be smashed and some cars overturned...

Since we have begun speaking about the "mob", let us make mention of those who despise the presence of any crowd at all. These are the intelligentsia, a very specific social stratum in Russia. Over the course of its history, the intelligentsia has changed, even in its national composition, but its orientation has always been the same.

The intelligentsia never lived well. At all times they were neither dear to the people, nor to the authorities. Among the simple folk, the dislike of the intelligentsia has a pathological character, because the people never considered intellectual labor to be true labor. The rulers despised the intelligentsia because they were always in the way and asked too many questions; while the bureaucrats were sensitive to their own inferiority. In any case, the intelligentsia in our land is not a Russian entity. Education came from Europe and the attitude towards the intelligentsia is the same attitude projected towards foreigners, which needs either to be planted in one's own land or is rejected because of incompatibility. They tried to create a hybrid worker-intelligentsia, but nothing came of it and the intelligentsia was left in its previous form. And as much as they tried to exterminate the intelligentsia, fumigate them like pests, they survived. Let us rejoice!

Russian bureaucrats are hardly unsymbolic of Russia. Bureaucracy has an expansive and glorious fighting history in Russia. Nothing could ever destroy the bureaucrat; he was victorious in all his battles.

Again, it all comes down to the great Russian laziness. An unwillingness to do one's own work, while placing the burden on the shoulders of others, is how the philandering starts. It is all as simple as an egg! Bureaucrats are immortal, which cannot be said of the intelligentsia, who despise laziness, and who are the sharp antipode of the people. But bureaucracy is an offspring of the people: it is their soul...

Here they are! The people of the limitless Russia. Those who carry the cross, that burden of mistakes and dead-ends. What have they created? What kind of cultural luggage have they accumulated over their thousand-year history?

Russian culture is unique. The spiritual, inner sorrow of Russia quaintly interweaves with European tradition. Culture is the strongest virtue of Russia, to this day. Unique Russian music and art... Speaking of art, Russia is the only country in the world today that has an official, strong school of realism. But these are just embellishments.

Russians are not logical, but naturally very deep. Natural depth, in conjunction with illogic, is also a national character. This is reflected everywhere: in literature, in art. Dolefullness, volatility, and sorrow are very characteristic of the Slavic race... The dead end in its historical past, which Russia stumbles on, is reflected in all art and ways of life. Russia is always under way, always trying to reach some goal. It seems to have arrived... Just a bit more and it would be there, but already another beckons from a different direction... Life in expectation of something far distant, so ideal that it is unimaginable... How many names that distant goal has had – glorious future, heavenly Jerusalem...

A totally grey winter day... Lost among the limitless fields, there is a city as if dissolved in unembraceable distance...

And from the sky, the fluff flies down – blindingly white winter fluff, called snow. The trees are frozen in expectation of something that will never come. Total quiet has poured over the expanse... And lost in the vertical dashes are countless bell towers...

The fluff flew from the sky... hiding temples conjured up by all the cunning of the dreamers. It came down on the timid panicles of the dry shore grass which shot through the young ice of the quiet river Kamenka...

A fantastic silver dove freely beat one wing, and scattered over the hills and lowlands uncounted churches, and beat the other, scattering over the fields, strong village houses, freshly built cottages and barns... He flew up, proudly observed the results, and fluff again circled in the skies and came down on the holy land where only magical birds and friendly lions live... "In the land of Suzhdali"...

And I thought: what was it like here, two hundred years ago? Nothing has changed since then, because this city is sleeping eternally. Hundreds of kilometers from here the regimes changed, the governments played devilish games of tag. All Russia was lost.

But Russia stayed here, in this city... Other people will always live here, people who do not care who has the power... another dictator, another president, or even the czar himself. The city will live as it lived through its thousand-year history, it will sleep as it has slept since the year of its founding... It stayed pure, left as an inheritance from that, Kiev's Russia...

So maybe we should not even touch this virgin tribe?

Russia, where are they all pulling you to? Some to capitalism, to the market. Others to communism. They pulled you to one side. Then the others came and said we were pulling in the wrong way... And Russia is still the same as it was one thousand years ago. The people never became citizens. They sleep ... just as this idyllic, quiet city cares not which way we will choose now, as long as it exists... And maybe this is the mysterious Russian soul?

Memorial to Minin in Nizhny Novgorod

Dobrohotov, Vladimir

THE PROPHETIC LEGACY OF PYOTOR
ARKADEEVICH STOLYPIN

> Love of the fatherland, first and foremost,
> is made up of a deep and passionate,
> not unrequited, wish for the good and for the
> enlightenment of the fatherland; a willingness
> to bring one's possessions, and life itself, to the altar...
>
> N.A. Nekrasov

Historical attitude, the understanding of one's place in the historical process – is one of the most important gauges of the moral culture of a society. During critical moments in the histories of peoples and nations, the contents of historical memory has a very noticeable influence on current events, on the behavior of the masses and of individuals; its effect is in the choices of the directions for a country's development. In our history, pages can be found which, when studied and analyzed, can help to solve the problems of modern Russia. April 14, 1995 will mark 133 years since the birth of one of the most famous political leaders of the 20th century Russian Empire – Pyotor Arkadeevich Stolypin.

This date is not a "round" number, but lately frequent articles and features on this man have been appearing in various publications and in the media.

The reason behind this is that the fundamental transformations of Russia, attempted by this wise politician, are similar, in many aspects, to the issues dealt with by the former Union of the Soviet Socialist Republic.

The beginning of Stolypin's political career was concurrent with the beginning of the political transformation of Russia, of which one possible result could have been the creation of a constitutional monarchy. The reform of 1861 had not only legally freed peasantry from "slavery", it also posed a number of serious problems of social and national natures, stirring up all the social classes of the population and forcing the monarchy to adopt a new approach to the questions of political authority. It was at this time, in Russia, that the formation of multiple political parties could be witnessed, each having its own goals and developing its own programs. In post-reform Russia, the agrarian question became the major concern of the government. The Derevnya (the countryside peasantry) was being impoverished – truly, a process of "the drainage of the center of Russia" was in effect. In St. Petersburg, and in other localities, there were constant conferences dealing with the agrarian questions.

In the capital there was a clash of two differing points of view. One was expressed by the Minister of the Interior V.K. Pleve, the other by the Minister of Finances S.U. Vitte. The former was mainly concerned with the preservation of the peasant *obshina*[1], which was always considered by the Czarist monarchy to be the foundation of "order" in the village, allowing itself to be sternly managed and ruled; and with the administration of economic policies directed towards the total state-support of large land ownerships which were going bankrupt. The state would have to become more directly involved in agrarian relations between peasants and landowners, with the goal of weakening the position of the peasants through police methods, and of defending the interests of the landowners. For a successful resolution of the conflict, it was suggested that the surplus of cheap labour in the landowner's holdings be transferred to Russia's undeveloped regions. The foremost goal of these efforts by the legislature was to protect the landowners who were going bankrupt from the growing peasant movement.

The second point of view was that of S.U. Vitte. He felt that the conflict between the landowners and the peasantry could be resolved by the foundation of capitalistic relations between the two, a capitalistic management of the land with the greatest importance placed on initiative and entrepreneurship. Vitte was categorically opposed to the Obshina land management, thought that the system should be based on private property holdings, and spoke out for the equality of the peasant class. According to Vitte, everyone on the land had to become landowners with equal rights: from peasants with minimal-hectare holdings to landowners of hundreds of hectares. In essence, the basis of the agrarian-reform program, which was implemented by the

---

[1] Obshina is an agricultural community of peasants, held collectivelly responsible by the state and/or nobility to work assigned lands which originated at the turn of XVII century

Emperor under the pressures of the revolutionary events of 1905, was laid down by S.U. Vitte, but he was unable to realize them in practice.

One of the key posts in the Russian government became the position of the Minister of the Interior, which, after the resignation of the Cabinet of Ministers, led by Vitte, was taken over by the young, 44-year-old governor of Saratov, P.A. Stolypin. After a short while, in June 1906, by the Highest Order of His Imperial Majesty, he was appointed the Prime Minister. During this period of political difficulty, Stolypin was faced with a whole complex of "hot" issues of utmost importance: internal politics, involving the interaction of the strong, sometimes contradictory inner political forces of the emerging democracy, and the centuries-old tradition of monarchy; national issues concerning the political freedoms being granted to such vassals of the Russian Empire such as Poland and Finland; military issues and others. But the core of the policies of Stolypin's government and the most important task of his life became agrarian reform.

In 1905 the fertile European portions of Russia measured 430 million hectares. 168 million of those were claimed as state, crown-domain, and church lands; 152 million were either owned or rented by the peasant Obshina, and 58 million belonged to landowners. The remaining 52 million were owned by 400,000 peasants, or by 85,000 city-folk who bought land outright.

Despite the political transformations in civil management, the judicial system, censorship, press and media, and others, implemented by Alexander II, and partially by Alexander III and

Nicholas II, the issues of land ownership became increasingly explosive at the beginning of the 20th century.

The political struggle which emerged in the first Duma (Congress of Peoples Representatives) between the supporters and opponents of the land transfers to private peasant ownership united, as strange as this sounds at first, ultra-right and ultra-left parties and blocks. The left insisted that, in the interests of the development of the class struggle in the Derevnya, there was a need for the total cancellation of private ownership by the peasants, while others on the left maintained that the reforms would mostly benefit the landowners and so-called *kulaks*[1] . (While the right demanded the preservation of the status quo). However, the majority of the peasant deputies supported the project which decisively rejected Obshina. On this matter, Stolypin's position was clear and defined: "While the peasant is poor... While he possesses no personal land property... While he finds himself in the grip of Obshina against his will... He remains a slave. And no written law will ever grant him the benefits of civil freedom." (Speeches of the First Duma)

This position became fundamental for all of Stolypin's activity in the agrarian realm. One of the most important and brilliant speeches of this young Prime Minister was his speech at the hearing of the Second Duma, May 10, 1907, in the Declaration of the Government on Agrarian Issues. Critically analyzing the varying views of the deputies of different parties on these issues, Stolypin did not reject a single suggestion or view, but instead gave a long-term prognosis of every position and point of

---

[1] *Kulak*, literally translated as "fist", is a peasant who lives separately from the commune.

view based on his knowledge of country life and peasant psychology. In principle, Stolypin pointed out four different positions on the agrarian reforms.

First of all, the left party sought to "destroy statehood with its landowner/bureaucratic foundation, and to create, on its ruins, a modern statehood designed along new cultural lines." The basis of the reform, in the opinion of the left, had to be the nationalization of the land. In his analysis of the particular moments of such policies, Stolypin stated that the nation would arrive at a state of affairs in which the interests of all classes would be subjected to a single interest while this one, even populous class would lead the nation to a "shift in the old values and to unprecedented drastic changes in social, judicial, and civil relations." He suggested that, even in the removal and dissolution of private proprietorship of the land, the agrarian question would remain unsolved because the "stimulus to labor, that spring which makes people work would be broken in such a scenario." Based on his deep analytic ability, Stolypin forewarned that this approach would lead to "everything becoming equalized, but only at a lowest common denominator." The Russian people have since found the truth of this statement in practice.

Another solution to the agrarian issue was offered by the Party of the People's Freedom. The acceptance of the "principle of an expropriation of the land" lay at its foundation, that is to say a redistribution of the land from those with massive holdings to those with very little. Moreover, this principle had to be in constant effect, destroying, as a result, the continuum of land ownership. Stolypin stated "nobody will apply his or her labour to the land, knowing that the fruits of these labours might be expropriated in a few years."

However, in the position of the Party of the People's Freedom, Stolypin had also noticed some important aspects. One of the speakers suggested that the peasants themselves should choose the forms of land use. "We cannot but welcome such a statement," reflected Stolypin. "The government in all its aspirations desires only one thing. We must loose the chains forced upon the peasantry and give it an opportunity to choose for themselves a way of land use which is most satisfactory to them."

Amongst the many speeches of the State Duma hearings, there were multiple calls for the expropriation of the land by the peasants. Stolypin categorically rejected such a solution to the issue, since, in his opinion, such a transformation would lead to the destruction of the state.

So, what was the position of the Stolypin government? His statements were not only declarative, such as: "The government wishes to see the rise of peasant land use, it wishes to see the peasant prosper, self-sufficient, because, where there is wealth, there is enlightenment, there is true freedom." His points of view were also specific and fundamental. First of all, it was a support of different ways of land ownership with an orientation towards a gradual transferal of land to the private sector. In his December 5, 1908 Duma speech, he stated: "In those regions of Russia where the individuality of the peasant has achieved a certain level of development, where Obshina as a forced union embodies an obstacle for peasant independence; it is necessary to give him the freedom to apply his labour to the land, it is necessary to give him the freedom to work, prosper, and to manage his own property; the peasant must be given the power of the land, he must be delivered from the servitude of the lingering Obshina system."

The second point was the creation of a land fund and the sale of properties to landless peasants on a preferential basis, in addition to extended preferential credit. Herein Stolypin strongly reiterated that the full solution of the agrarian question is a state problem, only to be solved by the state itself, which includes all the classes of the population, without any exclusions. "The opponents of the state", said Stolypin, "would rather choose a radical approach, free of cultural tradition."

And so, milestones were set and the path was defined. The majority of the deputies, and primarily those representing the peasants, supported Stolypin's position. However, the most difficult task of the realization of these ideals still lay ahead, a fact well-understood by the Prime Minister: "Having been involved in agrarian issues for about ten years, I have come to a deep conviction that a robust, long-term labor force is indispensable. We cannot dilute this issue, it must be resolved. Western nations have taken many decades to achieve these goals. We offer you a conservative, but effective strategy... "

The decisive action of Stolypin's government which began practical efforts even before the final legislation, resulted, in 1908, in the allotment of more than two million hectares of land to approximately 200,000 peasant families. The process was assisted by a whole complex of stimuli provided by the government: preferential credit by the Peasant Bank, the cancellation of certain debts, and the establishment of the right to disassociation from Obshina. Of course, everything did not proceed smoothly. Most of all, the sector of the poorest peasants became dependent on the so-called Kulaks and the large landowners. However, certain laws passed by the government resisted these effects. For example, the allotted lands could not be sold in order to pay debts, could be sold strictly to the peasant class, and only through the Peasant Bank. Moreover, there was a limit of six allotments per person.

But the most significant remaining obstacle to the reforms was the Obshina system. In many cases, the Obshina was practically organized on the basis of attitudes formed long-ago, which were not susceptible to change. For example, the Society of Elders and the Society of Peasants possessed the lands according to the old census. In these societies young peasant families had practically no chance of separating themselves from Obshina.

The importance of families turned out to be a central issue, one which received Stolypin's close attention and great care: "I consider it not only misguided, but also dangerous to substitute the established norms with vague ideas of sentimental socialistic quality."

One particular quality of Stolypin's approach to the solution to any state problem was an in-depth analysis of decision-making, a rejection of short term measures. The nature of P.A. Stolypin's government was to execute precisely, with reliability and stability.

Within 5-7 years great successes were achieved in the development of peasant land use and, as a result, in the output of agricultural production. In 1909 Russia exported across its

European borders 314 million pud (16 kilo measure) of wheat. That is to say, more than the U.S. and Argentina combined (266 million pud). Indeed, America's wheat export was in decline from 1907-10, while from 1908-12 Russia's exports increased. Russia led the U.S. in all sectors of grain and cereal production.

The program aimed at populating the best agricultural lands of Western Siberia, which belonged to the Imperial House, played an important role in the solution of the agrarian question. Over a relatively short period of time a number of villages, hamlets, and even smaller cities were founded.

After a trip through Siberia, in 1910, Stolypin wrote in his reports that the population had almost doubled, and that greater than a third of the population gain was counted in the years 1907-9. Such powerful growth in Siberia demanded resolutions to multiple problems, but the central issues were considered by Stolypin to be the establishment of good roads, railroads, the defense of the lands of southern Siberia, and the creation of, as we would say nowadays, an "infrastructure" which, in his opinion, had to include a complex support system and the establishment of good conditions throughout the region. The activities of Stolypin's government addressed all the aspects of the solutions to the concerns of the agrarian question: from the manufacture of railroad cars meant specifically for the relocation of peasants, to the strengthening of the defenses of the borders by establishing Cossack outposts.

The results of the agrarian reforms in Russia, started under Alexander II, "outlined" by Prime Minister S.U. Vitte, and practically administered by P.A. Stolypin, still are astonishing, sometimes even seem to be unreal. Here are some examples:

grain output in 1913 was 81.6 million tons (in 1926, 76 million tons), and per person amounted to 580 kilos (480 per in 1929). The consumption of meat, 1913 in Russia, per person was 88 kilos; an 87 kilo average in Moscow, 107 in Vladimir, 147 kilos in Voronezh. The average in the U.S. is currently 120 kilos. In 1912 the export of butter to England was valued at 68 million rubles which was twice the amount of gold taken in Siberian mines that year.

All of this, of course, made for the definite success in politics of Stolypin's government; and, together with this, undermined the authority of the majority of his opponents.

The leader of the Russian Social Democrats, V.I. Lenin underlined, on numerous occasions, the deleterious effects of Stolypin's measures: "Obshina, and its way of life, would certainly have been destroyed by capitalism. Stolypin senses this and is breaking it down." In 1908, in London, at the Congress of Social Revolutionaries it was decided that any success of the government in agrarian reform impedes the revolution. The action of the Social Revolutionary party was decisive and cruel – all out terror throughout Russia. Reading through the diaries of Alexandra Victorovna Bogdanovich, the wife of a famous general/member of the Interior Ministry, who lived throughout the reign of the last three emperors, one is astonished by the multiple incidents of terrorism: "February 27,1907: In Sevastopol. General Nekhlyudov had a bomb thrown at him. April 12, Ilyinsky, the murderer of L.P. Ignatiev, was sentenced to 15 years of forced labor... Maximovich and Shtormer spoke of this Gershuni a lot and I expect from him further terror. Maximovich mentioned another name, Trotsky, who had also escaped. He is also from the Worker's Union and from him we should also expect action. May 6: they are talking about the botched attempt on the life of the Czar."... and so on.

Even Milyukov had to admit that "through all our activity, we have gained a right to say that, to our great disappointment, we and all of Russia have enemies on the left. They are the ones unleashing the low instincts of human nature and are turning the Communist struggle into destruction; they are our true enemies."

In such a situation, as head of the government, Stolypin had to pay great attention to the fight against terrorism, which was taking on "Jesuit" proportions. In Kursk, for example, a bomb was detonated under an icon of the Virgin Mary, killing many churchgoers.

Terrorists made multiple attempts to kill Stolypin himself. An attempt on his life in August 1906 was especially heinous. The death toll of the explosion reached 27 people, including a young mother with baby, and 32 people, including Stolypin's daughter and 3-year-old son were seriously injured.

However, even these cruel acts of terror did not break the will of Stolypin, or his faith in a prosperous Russia. Unfortunately, the second program for the rebirth of Russia, in which Stolypin suggested, first of all, improvements in the ways the government ruled the country, never had a chance to come to fruition. In 1911, during the Emperor's visit to Kiev, there was an attempt on Stolypin's life, which resulted in his mortal wounding and death four days later.

Today, more than eighty years after his death, it is easier to value the actions of this brave and strong-willed politician and man, and to understand his meaning of Russia's destiny. It is easier to understand his thoughts, vision, and historical correctness. In his first speech in the State Duma, P.A. Stolypin said: "I want to forewarn that I do not allow for innuendo, and do not accept half-truths." This was his credo, from which he never deviated.

P.A. Stolypin belonged to the rare type of person that is a dreamer and a person of action. It is such people who are able to move Russia to great undertakings, to lead it down the difficult but straight road to great goals, to the prosperity and happiness of all of its citizens, and the long-suffering country as a whole. Now, with special importance, the words of the great Russian Prime Minister sound: "You need a great upheaval, we need a great Russia." (said to the revolutionaries).

Succeeding in the state coup of 1917, the Bolsheviks returned the Russian Derevnya to the Obshina way-of-life by creating Kolhoz (Collective Farms). They reestablished an ineffective system of agricultural production. This is why Russia faces the same problems which Stolypin faced in his time. The government and federal parliament, which rule Russia today, cannot, or perhaps do not want to, find the resolve to carry through the reforms which Stolypin championed. This is probably so because most of the deputies of parliament suffer from non-professionalism, which they have inherited from the Soviet era, when the teaching of state management was unsuccessfully directed at the kuharka (refers to the statement by Lenin: "Even the kuharka (servant cook) can manage the state.") Or perhaps the people's choices of today, when elected, forget the concerns of the state and become consumed with private affairs.

Today we can only dream of the appearance, among the Russian statesmen, of as great a leader as Pyotor Arkadeevich Stolypin. In my opinion, the famous Russian economist Grigory Alekseevich Yavlinsky is such an individual today.

Stolypin

Ezhov, Mikhail

WHAT IS TO BE DONE?

"Russia bends but does not break, while an understanding of their great destiny matures within the people."

I.A. Ilyin

Outline

I. From Russian History
  1. The Russian character
  2. Russia at war
  3. Czarist rule
  4. Russia, 1913
  5. Russian cataclysms

II. Lamentation
  1. Deviation from tradition
  2. Fragmentation
  3. Motives for reform
  4. Demographic crises

III. The Creation of Good and Truth
  1. Issues for educating the young generation
  2. The central role of the Teacher in Education
  3. The Fate of Russian economics
  4. Relations between nationalities
  5. What is to be done?

Night gives birth to stars, sunrise to the day, and, in the hidden depths of the past, lies the future. Do people remember the past as it deserves to be remembered? Do they know it in its true form? Do they perceive the history of their country in all its diversity? The historical path of our homeland is hard and thorn-laden. She has spent centuries in war and sedition.

The Russian soul has always been a mystery to foreigners. Even after hundreds of years of contact with the Russian character, they still cannot clearly explain to themselves the distinctiveness of the Russian nation. Throughout the process of history, peoples have gotten to know, and tried to conquer, one another. However, any attempts to enslave Russia ended in failure. Foreigners have searched for reasons for the invincibility of the Russian nation, clues to provide them with keys to victory over this unusual people. The source of the spiritual strength of Russia is the long history of the Aryan nation, one branch of which are the Russians. The other important factor which influenced the formation of the Russian soul was Russian land, i.e. the geographical uniqueness of the country. No other country in the world has such spaciousness, such slow, great, full-watered rivers, such open meadows and steppes, set on the borders with luscious birch groves. The lives of people, the forms and shapes of surrounding objects, by necessity create the consciousness of a person, his psyche, and therefore his behavior. The Russian character was formed, over millennia, under the influence of such majestic and quiet environs.

One more reason for its uniqueness was frequent warfare. Between 1055 and 1462 historians count 245 known invasions of Russia as well as external clashes. From 1240 to 1462 there was hardly a year free of war. Of 537 years, passing from the battle of Kulikov (1380) until the end of W.W.I, Russia was at war 334 years. During that time she had to fight against different anti-Russian coalitions. Moreover, oft-occurring reasons for wars were religious confrontations.

Despite the unending invasions and terrible military tension which burdened Russia from century to century, it grew and strengthened. In 1480 European Russia had a population of two million people (nine times smaller than contemporary France). In 1880 the number of citizens in the Russian Empire was more than 84 million (two and a half times the French population). Before W.W.I, Russia had 180 million and, if not for the social catastrophes which unendingly shook it over the period, in 1954, by demographic calculations, the population should have been more than 300 million. Such is the great life-force of the Russian people, which spread itself over the spaciousness of holy Russia. Terrifyingly and incomprehensibly (for the foreign, cold, external observer), she readily opens her secrets to any who inquire with love and hope, who come for support and help. The secret is simple: at the foundation of its external majesty and strength, Russian genius places many centuries of spiritual unity. The experience of personal piety ignited Russian soldiers on the battlefield with faith and courage, as it did the zealots in faraway monasteries, as well as the nobility in their management of state affairs. The words of the sovereign Emperor Alexander III come to memory, when on his death bed he told his son: "... I am interested only in the good of my people and the majesty of Russia. I tried to bring about internal and external peace so that the state could develop in tranquillity, and strengthen normally, to prosper and flourish. I bequeath upon you to love all that serves the good, the honor, and respectability of Russia." Nicholas II honored the bequest of his father.

Who remembers today that, before the beginning of W.W.I, taxation in Russia was the lowest in the world? That in 1913, the grain harvest was one-third greater than the United States, Canada, and Argentina combined? That Russia supplied 50% of the world-import of eggs, 80% of the world production of linen? The salary of an apprentice was 30 rubles, that of the qualified worker 100 rubles, while teachers made 200 rubles (salaries in Russia are traditionally monthly). One kilo of bread was 2 kopecks, meat 15 kopecks, and butter 45 kopecks. Russian merchants and manufacturers were prospering together with the country. The Russian factories could produce anything: from summer wear to submarines. Russia laid two thousand versts (1.6 km) of railroad annually. And in the 18th century, for example, there existed, for the first time in the world, laws protecting labor conditions (e.g. night labor by women and children was outlawed, limits were set on the length of the work day, and so on...) The code of the Empress Catherine the Great, which regulated labor conditions, was prohibited to be publicized in "civilized" France and Britain for being "seditious". The Russian code of law was the best in the world. Two years prior to W.W.I, the U.S. president Taft told Russian ambassadors: "Your Emperor has created superior labor laws, which no democratic state can boast of!" According to the national program of education, which was set long before the revolution, Russia was going to be a country of total literacy by 1923 .

But these plans were not destined to come to fruition. The cataclysm which began in 1914, undermined Russian strength, weakened it, and led to attempts to enslave Russia. All that awaited the Russian people was written in Dostoevsky's "The Possessed". His warnings were refused and went unheeded. Russian liberal society did everything to shake the foundations of the country and bring about the revolution of 1917. This is when the degeneration of the nation began. Mass terror, cruelty, and cynicism became the distinct features of Russian rulers. Those who could think, hold weapons, were arrested. Scientists, doctors, and priests were eradicated. And how many millions died of starvation! The battlefields of W.W.II are laden with Russian bones. And still Russia would not go to its knees. A careful look at Russian life bears witness to the fact that an original civilization came into being (whose high spiritual-moral values are becoming more apparent to us now) within a structure of existence where spiritual motives of life take precedence over material ones and where the goals of life are not things, not consumption, rather the transformation of the soul.

Russia, what has happened to you now? Is it true that the heroes and leaders of your glorious past, the heralds of your great destiny, have sunken into oblivion? The events of recent years show how much we have lost from the past. We forgot how to live by the laws of our ancestors. They did not dry up the swamps, which protect the land from freezing through; they did not cut down the woods as barbarically, even though they probably did not cut less. They did not alter the flow of rivers but, like the ancient Egyptians, made channels when necessary.

The diversity of the cultures of different peoples is the guarantor of humanity's immortality. But preaching the idea of the proletariat culture would have brought humanity into ruin. People's lives lost many traditions. Now the propaganda is primarily one of the culture of contemplation, of passivity, not participation in action, as has always existed in Russia.

Russia and her people were founded on the idea of centralization, the idea of the consolidation of Russia. And so it has been over the course of the last millennium. Russia has been able to play the role of a guarantor of peace and an egalitarian unity for its peoples. Russians are the cement which holds together the unity of this state; the unity between Yakut and Lezgin, Tartar and Venk, is maintained only through connection to the imperial body of Russia. The heart shrinks when looking at the thick lines of borders on the map, which split up the various republics. The separations of the Ukraine and Belorussia seem to be especially absurd. Despite the fact that the Slavic soul is alive, strong to its moral core, there is a trial of the soul, as in the great patriotic war, one which will bring not only victims. These trials burn lies, pretentiousness, and hypocrisy; renew the soul; strike sparks of honor and nobility. At this point I would like to quote the words of a poet, unfortunately unknown to me:

"Fire cannot be cold
  when sparked from the heart
  People cannot be free
  when they are apart."

I could not say it any better.

The introduction of pseudo-values into our soil has brought forth results in all aspects of life. A destruction of the notion of work as serving the good of the homeland is taking place. Under the banner of democracy comes all-permissiveness. Ideas of patriotism, duty, and honor are consistently exterminated from people's consciousness. There exists a propaganda of cruelty and violence; the sciences and education are being destroyed. The annual "flight of brains" (emigration) turns out big losses as well. It is with shame and bitterness I must admit that the choice of science has become an unattractive career. Never before has the figure of the scientist looked so oppressed and unprotected.

For any country, the rate of population growth and the problems of internal, national relations, have deep value. These, to a great extent, determine the strength and vitality of its statehood. Up to the revolution, Russia had the highest rate of population growth. So what do we have now? Entire regions of the country are dying out; only the elders are staying behind in villages to live out their lives. Life expectancy is down. Infant and mother mortality has been on the rise. There have been re-inflammations of viruses and diseases which had seemed to have disappeared. At the recent United Nations World Population Conference in Cairo there were 150 nation-participants, including Russia. The fact has been established that we have one of the lowest birth rates in the world, 9.4 births per thousand.

How did it come to pass that this entire country became a military exercise range for testing the durability and patience of people. This country is big and rich in black soil, gold, oil, gas and – poverty. Is it possible this is a result of mismanagement?

Right now the main goal of anyone who feels with his soul for this desecrated Russia, has to be the rebuilding of the continuity of Russian life. Earlier than 1,000 B.C., Zoroaster, in Persia, formulated ecological standards. He preached protection of the soil, reasonable procedures for grazing, and the protection of woods from clear-cutting. He taught that the material world of mountains, lakes, soil, sky, wind, and rivers is holy. A human and its environment are inseparably connected. The suffering of one brings the suffering of another.

But all of this must be taught in early childhood. The school has, and must play, its role as one of the foundations of the state and as a support of the moral health of the people. One of the main responsibilities of school is teaching the idea of the educational value of Russian history and an orthodox value system. The state can create a system of national (not nationalistic) education, in whose womb people will grow, people who are willing and able, first, to understand, accept, and preserve their spiritual, cultural, and ethnic belonging to Great Russia; and, secondly, to increase the spiritual, cultural, and material assets of the Russian state; people for whom "Russia and her destiny is a cherished holiness of their personal lives".

School teachers must teach an appreciation for the greatness and richness of Russian lands; love of the country and Russian history; love of creation; and the power of labor, its necessity, respect for it, its meaning, in order to teach the conviction that work is the well-spring of health and freedom. If the young generation had an inclination towards voluntary creative labor, it would perceive Russia as a limitless field of opportunity and there would be an awakening of will towards national prosperity and enrichment as the spring of spiritual independence and a flourishing of the different peoples. In this system of education the teacher is the central figure. He, or she, acts as a carrier of the moral origins and value-orientations of society: serving the fatherland, self-sacrifice, the priority of the spiritual over the material, responsibility for the destiny of Russia, and pride in belonging to this great culture and its heroic history. The moral substance of labor precludes the understanding of being rich as the goal of one's efforts. "Nothing brings as much conflict as the love of silver." said John Chrisostomos,... "Prosperity and poverty are judged not by amounts of material goods, but by ways of thinking."

The comprehension of the concept that material well-being is beneficial only when it is viewed as a means of spiritual achievement, helped form the Russian traditional economic way of life. Economic policies carried out today are directed at the destruction of this way of life.

Russia hangs above the abyss. Impoverished by infighting, vanity, and greed; suffocating in the grasp of economic crises, internal conflicts, and political quarrels; inebriated by the propaganda of permissiveness, violence, and debauchery, she mysteriously holds on above the abyss, in the dark bowels of which, the horrors of civil war and the final disintegration of the state await. The war in Chechnya shows that to fight one's own people is the last thing to do. In national relations within the country, there is a need to return to a healthy imperial practice which presupposes full (true, and not ostentatious) freedom of self-government.

Russia awaits help. What will stop our free-fall? Who will prevent the death of Great Russia, that living organism containing the lives of our ancestors of the preceding millennia? What is the reason for all our misfortunes? It is not simple to answer these questions. It was proven long ago that liberation from morality brings about the destruction of the individual and society. For almost ten centuries, Russian society, which is the incarnation of the idea of Rus, has been developing consistently and in reasonable harmony. This is how the inner stability and external defenses of the country were secured; it was a growth of the military and economic power of Russia. It seems to me that it is not the political or economic crises which are the main problems of today, but that philosophical and ideological crises are the most significant. On the one hand, former ideas, which united people, seem to be used up; on the other hand, amorality, brought to the rank of ideology, brings out, in the majority of Russian people, cynicism and rejection. Our salvation will not come before our acknowledgment and understanding of the danger – an understanding that must be shared by all. It is necessary to see this truth in all its nakedness; to look this hard reality in the eyes. It is especially important to mobilize, for the defense of Russia, all healthy, well-intentioned forces of society. Only if we can avoid these cataclysms, will we be able to speak of the prospects of our country's rebirth; about the ways in which we will find contentedness and peace; and a life of dignity and great goals.

Lapshin, Sergey

"TIME MACHINE"

...Esteemed Ladies and Gentlemen! Thank you for agreeing to accompany me on such an honorable and, I will not hide this from you, dangerous trial-run of the first time-traveling machine the in history of mankind. Yes indeed, it is "the time-machine". On this first run, we will not go just anywhere, rather we will travel into the past of our deeply-beloved (and deeply-despised by some) homeland of Russia. I urge you to listen to my monologues on Russia's destinies, which will be strengthened by what you are about to see. I caution you, this is just a trial-run, and to those who read this work... please do not be surprised if you see a red banner above the 16th century Moscow Kremlin with the slogan: "Decisions of the Czar-father to life!", or, in 1861, when we hear from "the Congress of the Serf's Deputies of the 12th hoarding"...And so I think we can begin. While various technical subtleties bring us to the starting point of our travels, to the 6th century, the time of the appearances of the first, relatively large Slavic settlements of the Slavin, Rusich, Drevich, and Tmurich, I want to express my point of view on the given historical period.

In general, Russia, in this period, as in the that era which followed, never had too much luck with its different rulers. The various principalities fought amongst themselves under their respective "sun-like" leaders, like children. Because the Slavs covered such a large area, from the Elba in the west to the middle Dnepr in the east, and from the Baltic Sea to the north, to the Danube in the south, these wars tended to be neither small nor harmless. In the hearth furnace of these difficult trials, the strong characters of the leaders were tempered, leaders who led their people down the path of progress. Just now, ladies and gentlemen, the year of 988 flashed by us. It was the year of the acceptance of Christianity in Russia, and the time of Svyatoslav, who was probably the first strong political personality. I ask you now to pay close attention to the year 1019, the beginning of the rule of Yaroslav "the Wise" (1019-54) and, with him, the appearance of the first code of law, "The Russian Pravda". The code was divided into three versions of increasingly descriptive detail, which allowed any Russian to choose for himself the appropriate rendition and follow it, which, I might add, is a very democratic feature.

Speaking of democracy, the principle of this form of state-hood is the least familiar to the Russian soul. Remember, over the entirety of Russian history, the seat of power was always occupied by one man or, a small group of people, supported by an appropriate bureaucratic apparatus.

"All these bureaucrats!", a classic once exclaimed. "No opposing army, no ruthless conqueror, has done our state as much harm and brought as much worry as they have. They are the only real force standing in the way of any progress, because they themselves are not susceptible to any progress." Why? Let us recall something: the bureaucratic apparatus of our state (and that of any other country) sprung up from... yes, exactly!... In reality it came out of the scribes and other segments of the educated public, and was selected by the Czar's chieftains and the priests, ... ever since the times of the pharaohs of ancient Egypt. Those were accepted to the position of scribe who were knowledgeable and shrewd, and smart enough not to climb to the very top from which one could easily fall. Generations of rulers used the services of these unstoppable soldiers of the bureaucratic front, who faithfully and steadfastly preserved the unchanging and untouchable nature of the system, which provided them with a living. Moreover, it matters not that he, the scribe, or bureaucrat, started his service in socialism, continues it into capitalism, and will end up God knows where. It is irrelevant to the bureaucrat which leaders or social structure he serves.

Speaking of rulers; all counts, czars, and emperors can be divided into two groups: those under whose rule something was happening, and those under whom nothing happened.

Ladies and Gentlemen, I beg your attention! After a lengthy procession of years, rulers, popular rebellions, and wars, we find ourselves at the beginning of the 18th century. Before us stands "the great persona", a man whom many historians place at the fore of Russian rulers. Before us – Peter the First.

In only a quarter-century he was able to radically change all of Russian life and send her along the most appropriate path of development for those times. Yes, I agree – he used very severe methods, such as cutting off beards (often by his own hand), blackmail (how else should one describe his telling the nobility that he would sell off their lands to foreigners, should they fail to give money for his reforms); further, we can list the building of a new capitol, the destruction of the Swedes in the Northern War, and the creation of a radically-new type of administrative, economic system of state-management – the Collegia.

When this great man died, Russia continued to move, by inertia, in the same direction, but at a slowing and more and more uncertain rate.

Rulers come and go as the river of time and historical development flows, sometimes slowly, sometimes more quickly, depending on which ruler navigates it at the time. If it is a liberal reformer, the river flies like a torrent over rapids, ever faster; if it is a reactionary conservative, the river slams into dams and obstruction, which, we should notice, the river nonetheless still flows slowly past.

And so our peoples developed peacefully until the well-known events of the beginning of the 20th century. What was the reason behind this global revolution? There are probably many reasons, although no one can give the definitive answer.

First of all, the majority of the merchant's families did not want the return of the monarchy, even though they would have been able to support it. The Nobility? – the nobility, at the time, was too weak and had no influence over current events. And, of the unpopularity of the Czar amongst the general public, we need not even make mention.

Then came the provisional government, which, in reality, illegally usurped the power and was partially supported by the military and mercantilists; it did not have any real foundation in existence, fully substantiating its name, "provisional".

In principle, any party, at this moment, could tip the scales in its favor. The most prepared, flexible party, full-of-initiative, turned out to be the Bolsheviks and... there was a total upheaval in the political and economic life of Russia.

There is only one thing the Bolsheviks failed to take into account. They were carrying out a revolution for, and with the help of, the proletariat. The peasantry, however, received a prominent, though far from preeminent, status, because the Bolsheviks thought they were satisfied by the famous Land Decree. But, did they not represent over half of the population? So, please, agree with me... the Bolsheviks were carrying out a political revolution, not a social revolution. We only experienced a true social revolution, and its consequences, after a long civil war. And only by paying the price of the "dictatorship of the proletariat" – great destruction and sacrifice.

I would like to make a further point: to put Ulyanov (Lenin) at the head of Bolshevism and the revolution is no insignificant mistake. Despite the great organizational abilities of Vladimir Ilyich, please agree that it was impossible for him to achieve the proposed measures on his own. By 1917, the ruling apparatus of the Bolshevik party already had a membership of more than a few thousand and decisions were not only made by Lenin. So, to praise, or to blame, Lenin, solely, is not acceptable. Lenin only fulfilled a unifying and controlling role.

And now I suggest, without further ado, that we proceed to 1985. Let me pronounce, literally, the painfully-renowned words which have been repeated on multitudes of T-shirts and baseball hats: "Gorbachev – perestroika". In such close association, we must examine the reforms, and the human being that declared to the world their beginning and their implementation.

These reforms did not lead to anything but a deep economic crisis. The bureaucracy remained the same, while the form of government simply changed its name. Even under the threat of death, I would fail to understand what the difference between the responsibilities of the president and the general secretary is, as well as that between the Duma and the politburo. And why was it decided that, with the car stuck in the mud, it would be easier to get out if the engine, wheels, and body were scattered in different directions?

Here, in my opinion, is the reason why our "states"/ex-republics have found themselves at such a disadvantage and in so pitiful a condition. The majority of them, after a very natural period of exultation, understood that changes had to be gradually implemented, that everything need not be destroyed, but saved rather to build on as an economic foundation. Instead, they received very advanced politics and lagging economics.

Even though we are now heading towards capitalism, I think that something absolutely new, never seen before, will come out of today's Russia. I am not looking for some kind of messiah to save humanity. In general, no single being could be separated from the environment. So, one cannot examine a single state independently of the rest of the world. At this point in time there is a striving towards the alignment of different countries into groups. It is not difficult to imagine what will happen later: the groups will unite and their numbers decline, while the group sizes increase, until the most powerful economic alliance unites all the rest and, softly but with determination, subjects them to its rule,... or presents them with such convincing reasons that the process becomes a willing one – there are many different, possible methods, but this is not the primary concern here. The most important thing is to have such a country or group strong enough to unite the rest. Right now it is the US.-European union which possess this ability. Russia, however, still can take their place if it stops emulating different styles and models, and instead chooses its own path. And, is it not easier simply to be oneself... ?

So, gentlemen, our travels have come to an end. Thank you for your attention.

Lenin's Square with Lenin's Memorial in Gorky, 1989

Marinin, Sergey

"POLEMIC NOTES"

"It is not enough to be born Russian,
One must be one, become one."

Ten or fifteen years ago nobody even imagined that it would be so difficult to reflect, in 1994, on this theme. The construction of this theme would have been different: one might have spoken instead of the "Soviet Union", or "the USSR", and the word "Russia" would have had a "backward" connotation, would have been pre-revolutionary, needing a "czarist-Russian" qualification. Our parents would have most likely drawn a breath of relief had they been asked to write such an essay at their final school examinations; back then everyone was proud of the homeland, she was universally loved, because, since the compulsory days of Oktyabryata[1], they had known:

"Oh, how wide my native country is,
   There are abundant woods, fields, and rivers,
   I know of no other country,
   Where man draws freedom with every breath."

---

[1] Literally translates as "Children of October" (October is synonymous with the October revolution)-- the compulsory league of young communists (ages 7-9)

123

And now we, their children, have found ourselves at the breaking point of history and are envious of those who had faith in the future, in principles (who believed in "something", as they used to say). Our generation has found itself in tragic circumstances; we have nothing to inherit from the older generation, since all spiritual values have been destroyed, even those of patriotic sentiment, and remain unreplaced by new ideals. This is why I find it difficult to write about Russia,... but I will try.

"The water stands still as glass,
and there is light in its depths,
And only the pike, like an arrow,
pierces the water's glass.

O native, humble view!
Birches, huts on the hills,
and reflected in the depths,
as a dream, there stands God's centuries-old temple.

O Russia – thou great astrologer!
As stars cannot be taken down,
Centuries pass, in the same way,
without touching this beauty.

As if this ancient sight
had been forever preserved,
in that soul, which guards
All the beauty of the past."

In these lines, the great Russian poet, Nikolai Rubtsov, gave the love of his big heart to the homeland, to Rus', which is in the soul of every Russian. The poems heal and help us stand strong in these cruel times.

Russia: yesterday, today, tomorrow... What does yesterday mean to us? It could mean five years ago, could mean seventy, or even five centuries ago... And what is Russia's today? A strange feeling is coming over me. Specifically: understanding the events of today presents a significantly more complex task than to understanding events in the past, of the 16th century, for example. One can only passionlessly record current events, since the understanding of them is "protested by the heart".

Here they are, the signs of our times: growing poverty, crime and robbery; bankruptcy; massive waves of political murder, which remain largely uninvestigated; "civilized" rogues, whose symbols have become rubber chewing gum and rubber billy-clubs; frenzied struggles for power, which are really just for a higher standard of living; and, also, endless numbers of refugees, refugees... Is it possible to remain silent in the face of this last fact, when it is the actions of certain pseudo-politicians who cause families to be torn apart, loose their homes, and turn against their neighbors of yesterday in hatred. Someone may reproach me – "oh, these are just emotions!" (today, emotions irritate, because people are cruel, with a leaden sparkle in their eyes, and a steady hand), but we are in an age in which feelings dominate reason. This is why I will risk boring you with a poem, which I copied from the newspaper, earlier this year (the author Panteleev, from Vyborg):

"Russian Refugees"

"They trod at the end of the 20th century,
having lost faith in the myth of human rights,
They struggle along through side-long glances,
the unfortunate children of Great Russia.

Why are our brothers punished like this,
sent into this hopeless, dark exile,
leaving homes behind, discarding all possessions,
Why do they receive this punishment.

Is it because they settled without suspicion,
from one end to another of this great empire,
Is it because former myths have been conquered,
Or is it because the ship has run-aground on the reefs.

Is it because borders are aflame with civil strife,
and Russians have become personas non grata?
And here they run, our regular folk,
as in the years of the Khan Baty invasion.

Oh, hide them O Russia!... in your limitless space,
Hide them in the branches of your tender birches,
Warm them, O Russia, with your generous soul,
Set their tables with simple food.

Give them refuge as you've always known how,
As you have done for so many non-Russian guests,
Accept them, O Russia, it will not bankrupt you,
since these are your own Russian people!"

This is all so true! Each one of us cannot but identify with the grief of a Russian, worried about the fate of his people.

So why should we calmly accept the statements of the army's "necessary station" in Chechnya? The main function of the army, known to us pre-draftees, is to defend the homeland from enemy attack. And since it is constantly underlined that Chechnya is a "subject of the Russian Federation", why, then, is it that our "artillery pounds its own"? (The poet of this last phrase, of course, had other events in mind.) For a year and a half, if one follows their logic, Chechnya was run by violators of the constitution; there was abundant counterfeiting, which damaged the entire Russian financial system (which is why butter costs, at least, 20,000 rubles per kilo); its drug business was becoming the "best in the world" (as in the Soviet lingo of the past), while the "fathers" of Russia, just observed and aimed their guns; and finally decided to restore order. Why should I consider it a restoration of "order" when, on television, I see crying women, the ruins of Grozny, and "peace-keepers" atop tanks, who chase away the journalists? Are these not the same "peace-keepers", who chased Vasily Belov away from the White House (Russian Parliament)? How can I, standing on the doorstep of independent life, prove to the wise people at the helm of Russia, that nobody ever conquered with the goal of improving the lives of those they conquered! You cannot prove to the populations of Karabach, Chechnya, or some other region, that those who shoot at them do so for the re-establishment of "law and order". In the same way, we cannot agree with the statement that the events of October 3-4, 1993 brought a victory of "law and truth". Why? Again, because they shot at people, while dissolving the popularly elected Parliament. Is it now the State Duma's turn? Since their membership still includes many of the same deputies, including V.V. Zhirinovsky... .

I often read certain newspaper reports, and my soul turns to ice (this expression has become a stamp... and there are no better words to describe it!) Here, for example, the Russian Vestnik of October 12, 1994 reports: "On April 24th, a day before the scheduled presentation of the "The Murder of Esenin", the poet and author of the book, I.V. Lystov, was murdered. He was struck in the forehead with a heavy object (similar to the crime at "Angleter", related in the book), and his body thrown in the pond." This is not an isolated sad event, which falls into the category of "unsolved cases"; how many more are to come? Meanwhile, many political leaders go to church, hold candles in their hands, speak to Alexii II, the Church patriarch, but, for some reason, forget the commandment "thou shalt not kill". Does it mean that goals justify means? What kind of goal is it that requires annihilation? It is popular to compare today with past historic events. There was, for instance, the period of "Smuta" (sedition) at the beginning of the 17th century; and some claim that something similar is occurring now in Russia. Peter the Great was intensely involved with the advancement of Russia, continually working to "chop a window to Europe", but he was impeded by reactionaries, in the same way they interfere now. Those, for example, who are against privatization are branded as being "against progress", and rejecting reform (the new minister of state property has recently declared that privatization should have been implemented differently – here are the red/brown opponents of reform!)

Respected scientists claim that history disallows not only the subjunctive, but also primitive comparisons of "time's passed" and "time's present". Yes, there was Svyatopolk[1] ("the Damned"), and Baty[2], the Kulikov Battle[3], and the famed "Smuta", and the Great Victory (W.W.II – the fiftieth anniversary of which we are about to celebrate). But if we attempt to find something in these events similar to today, we will find nothing. A vast difference lies in the meaning of the facts and the actions of people. What, for example, inspired the warriors on Kulikov field? It was the fact that they stood for the Holy Russia. How glad I was when I read the following words by V.A. Zhukovsky (which very clearly expressed that which had been unclear to me): "... there (in Holy Russia) lies our power, our all-encompassing borders, our state's virtue; here lies our memories of the lives of our ancestors, our internal folk life, our faith, our language, all that is truly Russian, which belongs to us alone, and cannot be found anywhere else... .that which only true Russians can understand." Zhukovsky wrote this to P.A. Vyazemsky from France in 1848. He defined the particularities

---

[1] XII century Russian ruler
[2] Mongol conqueror of Russia, grandson of Chengiz Khan
[3] First defeat of Mongols by Russian forces in 1380

of the Russian spirit and soul, buttressed by strong faith. Poet and citizen, Zhukovsky claimed that "our people have their own special God", since they have not only expressed faith, but also a "legend of God" as the "old partner of Rus", present to our ancestors throughout the times of their lives, good and bad, glorious and dark; in these words, our courageous and care-free avos (fatalist attitude) is joined with a strong hope for divine providence."

Not only Zhukovsky, but many other thinkers also claim that it is this faith in their own, Russian God which has determined the unique historic path of Russia. Zhukovsky describes it in this way: "Two major forces, originating from the same spring, have been, and continue to govern "her" fate; they will forever preserve her uniqueness if they, remaining constant in their essence, direct and determine her necessary historical development. These two forces are the church and the monarchy."

This is Slavophilism, which we have been branding with shame since 1917. But the reasons for confrontation between Slavophiles and Westernizers (in the 30's and 40's of the 19th century) centered not only around the rejection, or acceptance, of the western experience, but concerned the preservation, or destruction of the spirit of the nation. Why did the Slavophiles reject the western path of development? They were convinced that the west was ruled by egoism and dead materialism on which one cannot build commonweal, and Russian folk, who reject all this theorizing, remain faithful to the Church and Imperial power. Next followed thoughts, which, in my opinion, are becoming more clearly understood today: civilization exists in western Europe, but basic virtues are destroyed; Russia, on the other hand, has preserved these virtues, which will help in building our own civilization on the foundations of the Church and the monarchy. The latter will have to act in accordance with the laws which assure common rights to all. In this respect, the words of F.I. Tyutchev sound very realistic and confirm the existence of a faith in a unique Russian civilization, in Russian progress: "By mind alone – Russia is not to be known/ A common yardstick will not do/ She has a special, unique stature/ In Russia, you can only trust."

What is better, what is worse – following the unique ways of western development? History, I think, has answered this question. It happened that Peter's new innovations (he is considered a great reformer) collapsed immediately after his death. And this was not only because of the absence of the initiator of these reforms: the western model, in modern terms, could not take root in Russian soil. Shtoltses[1], with their pragmatic approach and energetic invasion of all spheres of life, have still failed to penetrate the souls of many. While Oblomov persevered, and I do not consider Oblomov to be a symbol of laziness and idleness; he has an impulse for action (he realized, however, that his actions were frivolous), and there is a delicacy and generosity in his big-hearted Russian soul...

What lies in Russia's past? I think that the dominant, underlying point which had determined the historic path of Russia, up to 1917, was an attempt to preserve Orthodoxy as the principle ideology of the people. Indeed, it was the Orthodoxy which could establish high moral principles, and make the society rich

---

[1] Shtolts and Oblomov are literary heroes of XIX century, representing enthusiastic German engineer and dissaffected Russian noble.

in spirit and justice. It is not in vain that Russian literature has given us great works in which "good", more often than not, triumphs over evil, and, in the converse cases, loss of faith is given as the cause.

So what constitutes this "loss of faith"? In order to answer this question, I will allow myself a recapitulation of the essence of Christianity (my conception, of course, has been formulated by the New Testament, our Church-fathers, extensive conversation with a certain country parish priest, and also by an article entitled "New Age Temptation", by Father Andrey Kuraev, in "Novy Mir", #10, 1994 (famous Literary Russian Publication), presenting many views, which cannot but be accepted by any Christian).

Now, all the "believers" (it is fashionable to believe) incorrectly think that the most important things in Christianity are the teachings of Christ, which is why most of their attention is paid to the Sermon on the Mount. But the true Christian would never call Jesus a teacher – for him, Jesus is a Saviour. Therefore, to be Christian is to understand that Christ died on the cross to save the people. Besides that, Christ always pronounces in his sermons: "Believe in God and believe in me. I am the light of this world, I am the bread of life." Therefore, he does not prophesy his thoughts, rather affirms himself as a personality. This is why the most important accusation against him was that "he makes himself God". Therefore, the life-giving cross, and individuality are the most important aspects of Christianity. The first concept always forces believers to do good for others, even to accept a torturous death, which Christ accepted. The second concept affirms God's personality – if it does not exist, there is no one to confess to.

This is how Christianity was understood by the Russia of yesterday. In this righteous country, sacrifice and confession have been glorified by ancient literature, the creations of Pushkin and Dostoevsky. Thusly, a chronicler writes on the death of St. Boris:

"... he told the priest to conduct the matins, and himself reads the psalms and the canon. As the morning prayer ends, he remains before the icon, still praying: "Lord, You have suffered for our sins. Allow me now to suffer for Thou. I am dying, not at the hands of my enemies, but by my brother's hand. Forgive him for that."

Gleb also sacrifices his own life in the name of his companions: "Brothers, if we do not fight them, they will just take me and deliver me to my brother. If we fight, we all will die. Swim to the shore, I will remain in the middle of the river."

Therefore, authority has always been a highest Truth in Russia – God. And, very clearly, two different truths were contrasted – God's (the path of mercy), and the secular version, that of deceit and revenge. Which was more prevalent? To answer this question, one way or another is, of course, impossible. Here we can cite one thought of A.I. Solzhenitsin: "And people always were greedy and often cross, but there was an evening peal that flew out over the village, the fields, and the forest. It reminded one that it was time to abandon earthly business and surrender one's thought to eternity. This peal, which is only saved now in an old psalm has kept people upright." The truth that is Christ has united all the separated folk (directing them to "single sky", in the words of Solzhenitsin), made them enduring and steadfast, defined the principles of the Russian military – "for the faith, for the czar, for the fatherland".

It is not by chance that, in times of trouble, all of Orthodox Russia could be moved by the words of those who dedicated their lives to God. The 14th century... the Russian people grow faint under the Mongol yoke, the abandonment of the Fatherland has reached its last limits, and stands on the brink of extinction. Then, through the example of his Holiness, by the heights of his spirit, Saint Sergii Radonezhskii, " raised the fallen spirit of the Russian people, awoke a belief in themselves and their strength, and breathed faith in God's blessing into them." – V.O. Klyuchevskii. He turned to the two monks, Alexander Peresvet and Andrey Oslyaba, with the following words: "The cross of Christ, which is printed on your vestments, will serve you in place of helmet and shield. In this way you will strike down the evil infidel!"

The battlefield of Kulikov on which Dmitry Ivanovich received the blessing of Sergii is known to all. The heroism of the Russian people on the field of Borodino is also considered a holy act, since it was undertaken for the sake of saving Russia (the soldiers said that they were unafraid to "lie their heads" for their faith and their fatherland).

As was previously mentioned, Russian literature was deeply concerned with the way to Christ. The way to Love and Beauty – and only that Beauty is the true one, which leads us to the Saviour, which raises us to the love of our neighbors, to come to peace with life. This is the Beauty, which F.M. Dostoevsky spoke of, and not of that which lies in the eyes of the beholder.

It is to such ideal beauty that the ways of Radion Raskolnikov and Mitya Karamazov lead. I believe that it is these ideals, and loyalty to them, which have blessed our national virtue, our national pride.

October 1917... What kind of Russia is it, past or present? The Church and Orthodox culture (Pravoslavnaya – "Righteous Glory") were destroyed. Events which F.M. Dostoevsky had forewarned against: "If there is no God, and no immortality, then all is allowed." This means that one who does not know God is filled with evil. (It is not for naught that the author uses the biblical story of the exorcism as an epigraph to his novel "Besy", "The Possessed".) In this novel (considered to be his weakest), many heroes realize this evil energy through destructive impulses; for example, Pyotr Verchovenskyi, and his accomplices, "Nashi"/ "Besy", nest in the absence of Christian criteria: "... the teacher who laughs with children, joking about their God and their cribs, is already one of ours. The students who kill peasants for the experience, are ours. The prosecutor who is afraid, at trial, that he is not liberal enough, is ours. Administrators, literators,... oh, there are many of us amongst them, even if they do not know this themselves!" These words of Verchovenskii are clear to us; by now we have felt them in our lives. It is they, "Besy", who now, to serve short-term impulse, substitute "full faith" in God with scientific paganism, which limits great spiritual demands.

"Besy" have had free reign: they have destroyed the intelligentsia (and now suddenly wish to reinstate them), and all classes and sub-classes were sent over the edge, especially peasants were affected, but their major crime consisted in the destruction of faith, the foundation of the state and the individual. A.S. Pushkin, a man of Righteous Glory, wrote that we owe our history and renaissance to the monks. "Unnecessary" replied "Besy", "No need for renaissance, no need for history. No need for churches, no need for priests – all this is intoxication (an opiate of the masses)."

Here is one more bogoborets[1] – the Grand Inquisitor: "In the place of your temple, they will build a new building. Once again there will be a great tower of Babylon... They will look at us in wonder, consider us to be gods... We will cheat them again (in your name), since we will not allow you to come to us. They will be glad to receive the sacred bread from our hands." In this novel (The Brothers Karamazov) F.M. Dostoevsky prophetically forewarned against the Grand Inquisitor's "secret" coming to pass. Those who say that they are with the people ("radeteli") are not with Christ: "... Listen: we are not with you, we are with him." "With him", in this case, means with "the great spirit", that is, the devil who tempts Christ in the desert. To every tenth-grader, who has studied the history of the Fatherland, the ways in which the Grand Inquisitor, and "the possessed", acted is clear. They took away the freedom of choice and faith – and are called "the liberated people"; they took away from them the bread they made; and then fed them that same bread from their own hands. All this because the Inquisitors secret is still alive. They are not with God, they are with the devil.

In the "Diary of a Writer", Dostoevsky says: "Without a spirit of love society could only be built on the salvation of

---

[1] One who struggles against God

stomachs. But "salvation of stomachs" is the weakest of all ideas. This is already the beginning of the end. This does not make for a healthy society, rather an anthill, devoid of church and Christ, with an undermined moral foundation... "

What is,... that is. What will be?

It would be insane for us to even attempt to predict the future. Who will undertake such fantasy? We are also fed up with these sci-fi novels on the era of the "great ring".

I only wish for our "unhealthy society" to be spiritually reborn. But we should not be so naive as to think the return to faith and the way of life of our ancestors can be achieved by a quick reconstruction of temples: this, we learned, is far from a reentry into the Christian world.

Still there is hope for a renaissance: Russian people are becoming spiritually enlightened, again turning to Righteous Glory and the Church, to the faith of their parents and grandparents, and to the behests of holy Russia. But the cleansing of the soul is a slow and difficult process, in Russia, truly, one must only trust:

"Who, then, told me, in the blizzard's mist,
 'The abandoned field is dying out.'
 Who told me that hope was lost,
 Who made this all up, my friend."

This poetry of Nikolai Rubtsov has a calming effect, and breathes hope...

Orlov, Vasily

AN INHERITANCE OF GREAT CHALLENGE

I, Vasily Orlov, 16 years old, put truly Russian questions to myself: "Who is to blame?" and "What is to be done?" I understand well that, for the last two hundred years, our national thought has not found a resolution to them, only finding dead ends or bloody answers.

I dare say that the reason for the lack of answers is specific to the Russian national character, which tries to solve everything from universal, cosmic positions. An initial impulse, which started from human love, was swapped for the love of human kind, and as a result, individuals were forgotten.

In our society it is customary to oppress the rights of the people for the good of the People in the name of the People. I insist that the appeal has to be to the individual, his concerns and feelings being that upon which the health of the nation is built, and not the other way around.

I have come to the conclusion that there is little chance to find the truth from official circles. But I am not a pessimist. My ancestors saved and gave me a holy gift (I am not ashamed of using this dramatic word) - A Russian, national, historical memory. It exists in my genes, it cannot be destroyed, it cannot be taken away and I will give it to my children.

Where does my family come from? There is a tale (unfortunately I cannot prove it at this point), that my family springs from the famous Perov lineage, which has given Russia statesmen, military leaders... and revolutionaries.

I can trace my family to my great great grandfather Dmitry Perov, who was the manager of the famous factory of Savvy Morozov. Thus, using my background of relatives passed away, and that of those who are still alive and well, especially my grandmother who is our connection to the past, I will start my story - about time, about myself, about my family, and therefore about Russia yesterday, today and tomorrow.

Russia, from the point of view of my family, is my great great grandfather - Dmitry Perov, a member of the intelligentsia, but most importantly, a carrier of the strong constructive impulse, the foundation of the strength of the country. These are the people who were called "the salt of the earth." Take a look! He was dressed in Western attire with a starched collar. He, and others like him, had a lot to lose, but had a creative impulse that was truly Russian, one of labor and creation. 1917 (the year of the Revolution) did not take money or mansions from them. Rather it killed the fruits of their labor, the labor which consisted of sweat, thought, effort, and the trust of generations.

For me, 1917 was scary because it attempted to crush that which was most sacred of the Russian genotype. Power was taken by those who chose not to remember their roots, or as it says in the Bible, prodigal sons. They destroyed the creative impulse of Russia because they could only destroy.

Thus came an hour of trial for my family. My great great grandfather immigrated to Italy, together with his eldest son Pavel, still holding onto the illusion that the parting was only temporary. Destiny and fate decided otherwise. The homeland remained unattainable forever. Never again, did he see his wife, Nadezhda Zaharovna Perova-Utkina, nor his daughter Anastasia, nor his sons Gennady and Alexey. Interestingly, the Communist Curtain over the country was not impenetrable. I do not know through which channels, through which good self-sacrificing people, but from far away Italy the letters from my great great grandfather came to Russia. How much light, and life was in the people to keep that small thread of connection alive? During the Finnish War, one of his sons Gennady, who went to war as a volunteer, joined his father through mysterious ways. I hope that one day I will read those Italian chapters of my family tree.

Those left in Russia were destined to go through much suffering. The second son of Dmitry Perov - Alexey - became the father of my grandmother. He died from starvation in 1929 and soon after his wife followed. Their children became orphans. They had to find the strength to live, and my grandmother went to work in the blacksmithing subdivision of the Gorky auto plant. Her husband, my grandfather, whom I am very proud of, was the secretary of the Komsomol. He, Osipov Anatoly Andreevich, together with his Komsomol subordinates, was building the Gorky-Shahunya Road. After that he worked as a manager of the casting subdivision of the Gorky auto plant. All of his awards were in the Museum of the Revolution. A book about him is soon to be published.

That was my mother's family line. On my father's side, my grandmother is a geologist. While working in Chukotka (Siberia) her group dug out a young mammoth, who was named "Dima." People wrote about it in the newspapers. After that she worked in Magadan with the electron-microscope to determine the presence of gold in different regions. She was the first Ph.D. among women in the Far Northeast. Her grandfather- my great great grandfather- was erecting beautiful wrought-iron fences modeled after the garden fences of St. Petersburg in the city of Saratov. My grandmother's sister, Kuzurman Diana Alexeevna, has thirty-three patents in chemistry. My mother, Orlova Elena Anatolyevna, has eleven patents. Also, my uncle has his own company. My cousin studies at Nizhny-Novgorod University, in the Department of Managerial Economics. My aunt has a Ph.D. and she is not even thirty yet; she already teaches in Vladimir Polytechnic Institute.

Why did I write all of this? Because Dmitry Perov left behind his descendants even though he left Russia. I am also his descendant, and I am not alone. We, his descendants, are the future of Russia. Savvy Morozov had sixteen managers - can you imagine how many descendants.

There are many of us, and there are more and more every day. Russia was a rich country. It had many entrepreneurs. For Russia, the day before yesterday was good, therefore tomorrow will be good as well because near-sighted politicians will not be able to destroy the Russian national memory. No wars or revolutions will help them!

As I write this, I am overcome by a strange feeling of how everything is mixed up in me: pain, horror and unacceptance of 1917, and the pride of my grandfather who faithfully believed in Communism. Foreigners would not understand, but I know an answer to this riddle. My great great grandfather Dmitry Perov, manager of the Morozov factory, and grandfather Osipov Anatoly Andreevich, Secretary of Komsomol Committee of the Gorky car plant, carried within them the Russian creative impulse and a holy faith in the future of Russia.

I, living at the end of the twentieth century, do not want to be their judge. I accept my past as it was, but I want to build the future myself, in such a way as to not shame my grandparents or my great grandparents or my descendants. I want to finish with the famous words of F. I. Tyutchev:

"By mind Russia cannot be comprehended, by average measurement it could not be measured, it has its own special way. One must have faith in Russia."

Osokin, Maksim

LAND DISTRIBUTION FROM SEDITION TO SEDITION: THE ETERNAL QUESTION OF RUSSIA IS THE QUESTION OF BOUNDARIES

A major factor in Russian history is the colonization of the Eurasian lands, to which all other issues are intimately connected. Russia's history can be divided into periods observing the movements of its peoples. These periods are stages consistently spent in the acquisition and development of lands until finally, by virtue of the natural population growth and the incorporation of foreign peoples, Russians spread over the whole Eurasian plain and even overflowed beyond its boundaries. These periods are periods of semi-permanent, stationary settlements, which interrupted the migrations. On each of these stopovers life was restructured. I will name these periods, pointing out the governing political and economic facts in each of them . I shall also describe the regions of the plain populated by the Russian peoples during the particular period – not the entire population, but its principal mass, which determines the course of history.

The development of the Russian peoples can be traced from the 8th century A.D. on. Up to the 13th century, the main mass of population was concentrated on the middle and upper Dnepr and its tributaries, and its historical waterway, the Lovach-

143

Volchov line. At that time Russia was politically developed into separate, more or less self-contained regions whose political and economic centers consisted of large commercial cities. The political separation of land, under the leaderships of the cities, was a political factor in this period. Trade of forestry products, hunting and trapping were economic factors. This was the Rus of Dnepr, the Rus of city-states and trade.

From the 13th to the middle of the 15th centuries, at the time of the break-up of the Russian nation, the main mass of population was concentrated on the Upper Volga and its tributaries. This mass remained politically separated, not in the city spheres of influence, but in the county realms. The subdivision of the Upper Volga Rus, under the power of the nobility, was a political factor in this period; while the agricultural exploitation of the plain through the means of free peasant labour was an economic factor . This is the Upper Volga Rus, a period of appanage principalities – free peasant agriculture.

From the middle of the 15th century, to the second decade of the 17th century, the main mass of the Russian population, from the Upper Volga, disperses to the south and east over the Don and Middle Volga Blacksoil regions, creating a new branch of the nation, which grows beyond the boundaries of the Upper Volga. Growing geographically, Russian tribes joined, for the first time, into a single political unit under the power of the Muscovite ruler. Therefore, the political factor of this period is the unification of Russia. Economic factors remained the same as previously. This is the Grand Russia, Muscovite Russia – czarist Boyars, military landownership.

From the 17th to the 19th centuries, the Russian nation spreads from the Baltic and White Seas to the Black Sea, the Caucasus mountain range, to the Urals and beyond. Politically, almost all the regions of the Russian nation joined under a single authority. This Grand Russia is joined by White Russia and New Russia. This political unification is the main political factor of the period. A major economic factor was serf-based agriculture. This is the period of the Great Russian Empire.

The major nerve of Russian historical process is the perpetual movement of colonization. The struggle for territorial and national self-determination presented very difficult tasks and required extreme measures towards their solutions. It is not only because of its unyielding nature that the great Russian tribe had to fight to acquire a cultural soil... for example, in the 15th century the wooded expanse of the northeast was populated by Finnish tribes and the Middle and Lower Volga regions were ruled by the Tartars.

The international position of the Muscovite state was extremely precarious and tense, since the existence of the Great Expanse required, for the solution of the issues brought about by the historic/geographic position of Russia, an enormous reserve of strength and means, which obviously were more than the population could produce. The eternal tragedy of Russian history is the inability of the population to satisfy the continuously growing national and state needs, and has defined the particularities of the inner state structure. Moscow's center was governing a very large country of thinly spread population, which had poorly developed material and spiritual cultures. To ensure the means necessary for serving the Czar's affairs, the central power could only achieve these ends by consolidating, in its hands, all the forces of the populous. The development of the unchecked autocracy became a necessary tendency in the political evolution of the Muscovite rulers.

Russia has been a primarily agrarian nation throughout its history and I will now examine agrarian relations in each of the periods. In 16th century Russia the land, which was populated by the peasantry, was divided into three categories according to different types of ownership: church held lands, lands held by the service classes, and Czarist lands. There were no other landowners because no peasants owned lands. The position of the peasant in the 16th century was as such: the majority of the class consisted of small scale, unstable workers of the land whose holdings and households were rented; who settled the land and labored using borrowed capital and who, under the weight of the demanded payments were tempted to limit, rather than expand their costly holdings.

Over the course of the centuries our history created a wandering peasant class, who worked the land of others, using other's capital. The historic issue of Russia's future was the creation of a settled peasantry, employed on lands to which it had strong ties. The vagrancy and landlessness of the peasantry brought about the fact that, in the 16th century, the majority of the peasants on the estates of large owners were tied to the land by loans and were in danger of becoming bond slaves (which was detrimental to the state, since slaves do not pay taxes).

Burdened by all of the state taxes, the peasants were giving up their work on state lands, and instead were renting undeveloped lots and consequently hurting the state treasury.

This forced the state to attach the peasants both to the state lands and the lands of small landowners, so as to prevent the larger landowners from enticing the majority of the working class. Later, the government sought to make this attachment universal, which, in effect, stopped the shrinkage of the state's agricultural holdings. These measures multiplied the number of peasant escapes which forced the government to increase the power of the landowners over the peasants. But, at the beginning of the 18th century, there was an increase of peasants who became servants, and the sale of which, without land, avoided taxation. To counter this, the government brought an individual poll tax into being. The peasant became personally attached to the landowner who was responsible for him to the government, thus making servants and peasants equal responsibilities. The institution of the poll tax brought about great economic results. Thanks to it Russia began improved use of its lands.

Therefore, with the increased economic and legal dependency of the peasants on the landowners, and support of government decrees (for example, the decree of 15 97) serfdom came into being in Russia. Serfdom embodies the right of one human to the life of another based on legal acts without any relation of the serf to the land – the right which gave the serf to the "private power and ownership" of the noble.

With such an extent of noble power, Russia experienced a large development of trade industry by serfs with and without land; there was an establishment of price structures – through the state and by the nobility. The peasants were sold singly, in families, as entire villages, with or without land, families were split. The power of the nobles increased over the serfs, but the previous state obligations became more difficult due to the responsibility of state taxes and the welfare of the peasants, especially in the years of bad harvest, etc. Such forms of ownership had not ceased to exist, even after the law of 1762, which granted freedom to the nobility, canceling their state service. This is why the events of the 19th of February, 1861, came ninety-nine years later.

Having been freed from state responsibilities, the nobility envisioned becoming the class of ownership and the managers of the country's economy, but because of serfdom, could became neither. Therefore, the nobility was gradually turned from being landowners to becoming serf overseers. With such a position of the landowners in agriculture, serfdom gave a wrong direction to the development of the economy of the noble's estates. Each need of the nobility was satisfied by increased taxes on his peasants.

Serfdom had negative effects not only on agriculture, but on the economy as a whole. It slowed the geographic expansion of agricultural labour. Because of the circumstances of our history, the agricultural populations were always concentrated in the central regions, working the less productive soil, since they had been chased, by Russian enemies, from the southern Russian black soil.

The system of serfdom held back the growth of Russian cities and towns and the development of urban trade and industry. Each well-to-do landowner had attempted to have his own tradesmen in his village. Therefore, the serf-tradesmen acted as a dangerous competition to the urban, industrialis tradesmen. The landowner, by his local means, satisfied his needs. When this failed, he went to foreign stores. Therefore urban tradesmen lost the most profitable and valuable customers. On the other hand, the ever-growing oppression of the owners limited peasant cash holdings. The peasants did not buy or order in the cities and consequently deprived urban merchants of cheap, but numerous customers. Finally, serfdom had a negative effect on the government's economy. State needs were not satisfied by peasant taxes, which brought about a growing necessity for reform.

The first step towards the dissolution of serfdom was settling the issue of the state's peasants, which meant equal distribution of equal land parcels, transferring the taxes from humans to the land, the creation of local schools, food stores, agricultural banks, etc. This was an example by which the noble's peasants could be settled, following the dissolution of serfdom. Catherine the Great deserves to be mentioned as the first leader to bring about open discussion on serfdom, by creating a State Commission for the creation of proposals for peasant life reform. But she did not achieve much besides this. The resolution of the issue was begun by the law of April 5, 1797, according to which, the noble could require from his peasants only three days of labour per week, allowing the peasants to use the other days for their own labour, making them payers of state taxes. The law on Free Cultivators was a second major step in the same direction: It allowed all nobles to free their peasants, either by family or entire village, with or without land, under conditions approved by both parties. Practical implementation of the law was rather limited, but its principle concept was extremely important; since the major conditions of such separation were the relinquishing of land under free agreement.

On these foundations, the Decree On Peasants liberated them from serfdom on February 19, 1861. By this decree, the nobles, while retaining ownership of all of their lands, had to give the peasantry certain areas of usable land for which the peasants had to carry out certain obligations. During the period the peasants were termed "temporarily obligated".

This reform was not completed under the rule of Alexander II. The land, retained by the poorest of the nobles after the liberation of the peasants, began to noticeably disappear as it was transferred into the hands of other social classes. In order to slow down their loss of land, in 1885, the Nobility Land Bank was established. By the Law of December 26, 1881, a necessary buy-back program was implemented in all the inner regions. Beginning on January 1, 1883, a necessary relationship between landowners and peasants ceased to exist. The Law of May 13, 1886, allowed the extension, over the course of many years, of unresolved buy-out debts of peasants. The Law of March 12, 1903, canceled the mutual responsibilities for state and federal taxes. Finally, the Manifesto of November, 1905, canceled all the peasants' debts for the lands in their position, starting from January 1907. The end of buy-out operations gave the government the ability to take the first steps towards the liquidation of the largest landowners.

Even a cursory glance at the distribution of the land fund in 1905 bears witness to the fact that the reforms of Alexander II were not carried out. After the abolition of serfdom some landowners/dvoryane (nobility), under the newly created conditions, would have been more than happy to sell their holdings which became a burden. But there was almost no one to sell to. Part of the land went from the hands of the nobility to the hands of the recently successful merchants and industrialists, but this, in no way, diminished the scope of the land needs hanging over the country.

The causes of these great needs were the ramifications of the obshina system. The allotted lands were divided among the peasant obshinas, each one having a set acreage of arable land – a kind of locked castle.

During the beginning of the rule of Nicholas II, many appointed committees were engaged in the study of the agrarian problem and were seeking a positive alternative. Meanwhile, time would not indulge their slow progress. It is better to conduct reform in peaceful situations, as opposed to times of rising revolutionary sentiments. Such was the conviction of P.A. Stolypin.

The plan of Stolypin's reform was to release the peasants from the obshina system and to create independent farmers. Stolypin experimented in Saratov, as he was the governor of the region. The results surpassed all expectation and, in the summer of 1906, Stolypin was named the head of the government.

The reform began in 1906, by the decree of November 9, 1906, which gave the peasants equal rights.

Without robbery, violence, or expropriation the size of pomeshiks' (landowner) land holdings slowly diminished, as did peasant land needs. There was support for the peasants, by the Peasant Bank, who were moving from communal villages to homesteads.

Let us underline some important results. In 1917, 40.8% of heads of household exited Obshinna. Concurrently with this movement, a natural and unavoidable division in equality within the peasant classes arose.

Thusly, at the moment of revolution, needs were satisfied for only a portion of the peasantry. Nevertheless, the effectiveness of the reforms was obvious: the agricultural output of the country grew by 14%, between 1906-1915. The authorities aided this process by mass-importing better breeds of livestock. Peasant land-management inventories improved with the appearance of tractors and other means. Russia became a grain-exporting nation.

After the revolution of 1917, decrees were issued negating all forms of private ownership. These Communist decrees supplemented the decrees of the Sovnarcom (Soviet People's Commissariat). Similar meaning was contained in the factual negation of the land decree, which had assured the Bolsheviks the support of millions of peasants and soldiers. Instead, on February 9, 1919, a law was passed, by the VTSIK (Central Russian Implementation Committee), "for the socialization of land".

This law created unmanaged, unowned land, and declared that the land was "being transferred for the use of all working people". This law contained nothing on the forms of land usage. The land decree of VTSIK, of February 14, 1919, "on socialistic land management, and the methods of the implementation of socialistic land use", stated that the land was under the supervision of the Narcomzem (People's Land Commissariat). In 1918, the country's economy had collapsed, and a class of land tenants was created; while, in the absence of owners, productivity fell. From 1927-30, all-encompassing collectivization took place, the class of landowners was eradicated, and Russia returned to the Obshinna system.

For the next seventy years, following 1917, no land reform took place. During this period, collective land use was the only system.

During the last few years, beginning in 1989, far-reaching land reforms have taken place in Russia. The Land Code of the 1990's declared a new class of land owners. The Land Code established three types of land ownership: common-divided, common-undivided, and private. In particular, on October 27, 1993, a law "on the regulation of land relations, and the development of agrarian reform in Russia" was issued. It states: "Citizens, legal entities (corporations, trusts), and landowners have the right to sell, inherit, give, mortgage, rent, exchange, and also transfer land space, as venture capital, to corporations and partnerships, including foreign investors." The right to transact in land is hereby granted only to owners.

The Nizhny-Novgorod region is the leader in land reform. For example, each rural citizen is allotted a land plot, which he/she can manage. New farmer homesteads, cooperative farms, etc. are forming. New systems of land registration have been created. The Nizhny-Novgorod model is similar to Stolypin's land reforms. It seems that, in the near future, this model will become pervasive in Russia. Russia will return to its pre-1919 condition: all will return full circle.

Podnebesny, Aleksey

RUSSIA IN THE TWILIGHT

"Russia, where are you racing to?
Give an answer. She answers not... "

N.V. Gogol

Countless words have been spoken about Russia; less and less "blank spots" are left in her past. Our history is extremely rich in dates and events and seems to be governed by some strange controlling factor, the understanding of which is probably only possible through solving the riddle of the psychological make-up of Russians, if you will, the Russian soul. In my essay I will attempt to find common factors characteristic to Russia today, a country in the transitional stages of its historical development. Is it not true that such transitions, periods of extreme national activity, fully reflect the somewhat hidden features of "quiet" everyday life? They also help to understand other features, or national characteristics, which are stable under any political cataclysm. All these factors make up the rich historical heritage which has been passed down from generation to generation since ancient times, from fairy tales and legends, to archival documents. As is known, "The fairy tale is a lie, but there is a lesson for the fair youth". In the days of old, people better understood this maxim and tried to avoid the mistakes of their heroes, while repeating their successes. Nowadays, massive amounts of information are within people's reach; the colossal experience of previous generations has been accumulated. It would be a shame to not, at least, attempt to make use of it.

Unfortunately, it sometimes happens that we act first and think afterwards. And when we reflect, we notice the extraordinary similarities between past and present. This is where the idea of "the wheel of history" (of all returning full circle) finds its origin. Analysis of situations, from an historical perspective, might predict ruinous consequences . As for the Russia of the past, the Russia of today is characterized by the fact that the decisions, which later cardinally influenced the development of the country, are made by the ruling elite, oftentimes spontaneously, without taking differing points of view into account. This is what leads to negative results.

In predicting the future of Russia, while considering her current state of affairs, it is not worthwhile to think only of the past. Special attention must be paid to today. Many of the great minds of our homeland, while predicting for her a radiant future, have often forgotten about her present. "Russia will awake!", "We will build communism in twenty years!", "Stabilization will arrive sometime in the 90's... " Further examples of such slogans could be given. And how about the well-known foreign sayings that Russia is a great empire that will be reborn again? But what is surprising is that this is not the first century in which Russia has listened to these voices. The 17th, 18th, 19th, and 20th centuries were are equally important periods in this respect. It seems that the desired perfection is reached: emancipation from the Tartar yoke, the unification of Russia, expelling the impostors (the Poles), cutting a window to Europe, victory over Napoleon, Hitler... but at every stage, after time passes, the words about the 'radiant' future begin to sound again. This, of course, can be explained by the characteristically human struggle for perfection. Only, this 'struggle' has lasted too long. Sounds absurd, does it not? But our lives are full of absurdity. In the search for new ways of development, our society has possibly veered too far off its course, at the end of which, this so-called "perfection" supposedly awaits us. While we have not yet reached this destination, we at least have a goal to strive towards. As far as faith is concerned, we, of Russian descent, have never lost it. Is it not true that the best representatives of the Russian nation, politicians, writers, poets, predicted for her a great future, thought about her destiny, and believed in the necessity for changes? During the 18th century, one finds the first literary works calling to attention the abuses committed in the fatherland, they also contained directives towards the search for new ways of development for Russia. Why specifically in this century? Because, in the 18th century, there arose, in Russia, the question of how to further develop the country. The eternal argument of the Slavophile and the Westerner came into being. The noble youths, who received European education under Peter the Great, understood the impossibility of developing a modern society, while preserving the institution of slavery – the "new Russian thought" was born. This "thought" underwent further development in the 19th century. In other words, the emergence of such mindsets is brought about by change in the socio-political environment, which is lagging in Russia, as compared to western Europe, by almost a century.

But why was it so difficult to bring this "thought" into reality? The Decembrist's rebellion was defeated. As is well-known, it was doomed; the rebellious nobility was estranged from the people, for whom they undertook their noble cause. Peaceful attempts to reform the status quo also failed. Is it not true, however, that the reforms proposed by Speransky could have prevented the rebellion. In reality, all was halted, or dashed, at the blind wall of misunderstanding. Here we must take notice of the special feature which is characteristic of our state and is threatening to become a feature of the national character. This was highlighted by Gogol: "Russia has two misfortunes: fools and rogues." (direct your attention to the former) This was also noticed by the turn-of-the-20th century writer, V. Gilyarovsky:

"Russia suffers two calamities,
   On the bottom, the power of darkness,
   On top, the darkness of power."

Truly, only a few representatives of the simple folk (Lomonosov, Kulibin, Shevchenko)[1] were able to reach a high level of knowledge, and become truly great people. The majority, meanwhile, remained a dark, inert mass, unwilling to accept any changes, which threatened the even flow of their lives. Only an extremely powerful pressure could force this mass to

---

[1] Lomonosov is considered a father of Russian science, Kulibin is an inventor, Shevchenko is a Ukranian poet

move. This is how the elemental peasant uprisings of the 17th and 18th centuries (under leaders Bolotnikov, Razin, and Pugachev) came about. Achieving contemporary success, they were later easily subdued by the authorities, since they lacked programs of action, and only had the goal of revenging insults and degradation. Disturbances burnt out, the steam from the kettle was released, the rebels were executed, and life returned to the previous state. People held on to their positions, afraid to slide into worse. Yes, they desired reform, because life was full of hardship; but they wanted immediate changes, without long transitions, during which there is the possibility of complication. Reform, with its long-term perspective, could bring about disobedience and anarchy among the people. And this, for example, is how the land reform of Baron Vitte failed.

On the other hand, progressive thought scared the ruling elite and its surrounding multitude of bureaucrats. As in imperial Russia, and in the U.S.S.R., the authorities and the bureaucracy were always the impassable obstacles to all that was new. Even liberally-oriented Alexander I was scared to bring about state reform directed at the transformation of the half-enslaved Russian society into a more democratic one. Only the direct threat of revolution forced Alexander II to free the peasants from serfdom. The authorities tried to reach this success through old methods. They did not need any new ideas. Without a trace, scientific discoveries and technological improvements disappeared in the bowels of the bureaucratic machine. The Russian inventor, Polzunov, from the Urals, invented the steam engine twenty years before it was perfected in England; but the proprietor of the factory, where it was tested, preferred to utilize traditional labor, afraid of extra problems with the mechanism. The authorities also failed to notice the new invention and, in the near future, Russia had to purchase similar equipment for its industry from outside its borders.

In 1911, G. Kotelnikov invented the first parachute. The invention was rejected by the military as "unneeded". In the years of W.W.I, the czarist government paid foreigners many thousands of rubles for the license to manufacture parachutes at their factories. And how many ideas have been destroyed by bureaucrats in our recent past, hidden in the KGB archives? All scientific potential was directed to the needs of the military industrial complex; and, due to fear, the lag-factor in the production of consumer products and appliances, was greater than ten years. While Americans were starting to use VCR's, we were listening to reel-to-reel tape recorders. When "they" began to develop computer technology, as the world spoke of the "Japanese miracle", we had only 15% of our factories fully-mechanized. However, it is a fact that TV and radio were invented by Russians; but V.K. Zvorykin had to develop his creation, which laid the foundation for the modern television, in the USA.

The following event is known. It happened at the Chusov metallurgic factory, which supplies the metal strips, used in truck suspension springs, manufactured in Minsk. Women workers went to the plant engineer saying: "It is too heavy for a pair of us to lift 85 lb. strips!" This seems at first to be a simple problem. By mechanizing the workers' labor, their strength can be dramatically increased. But no! Why should we need mechanization with all its troubles of implementation... It is easier to decrease the weight of the strip. And representatives of the Minsk plant tried to prove in vain that by lowering the weight of the strip, the reliability of the suspension would not be compromised. The weight of the strip was lowered; they were indeed heavy. This is an example of "technical calculation." This is perhaps why (the described situation was characteristic for many of our factories), in the 70's and 80's, Russia was associated, in America, with "baba", a humongous woman in work clothes, holding a sledge hammer. Indeed, manual labor, especially that of women, was widely used here at the time when robots were coming off the pages of science fiction to help man with his labor. Unfortunately, these robots were mainly being used in Japan and the U.S. At the same time, our poorly mechanized, unproductive labor force had to provide for the growing spending of the Communist Party. Extensive utilization of resources (including labor resources) led to the weakening of the economy and a dependency on the export of raw materials, especially crude oil.

About the same situation was in place in Russia at the beginning of this century, just before the Russo-Japanese War. We lost that war even though Russia was considered the strongest world power at the time. The loss of the war against the Japanese revealed the economic and technological backwardness of the Russian Empire as compared to the leading western nations. In the conditions of extreme imperialist competition for spheres of influence, such backwardness was very dangerous. There was a need for change; normal development of the country under the monarchy was impossible. The revolutions of

1905 and 1917 came as a result, and brought radical change to the existing order.

In 1979, the Soviet Union started the war in Afghanistan, which ended in 1988-89. During the 1970's there were two superpowers in the international arena: the USSR and the USA. In 1973, America, under the pressure of the United Nations, had to pull its troops out of Vietnam. When the USSR started its campaign in Afghanistan in '79, it was really fighting a war with Afghanistan, and the US, who armed and supported the Afghan Mujahedeen (as did Pakistan and Iran). The Soviet army in all its glorious strength could not overpower the small bands of the Mujahedeen. The war continued for ten years, brought both countries great losses, and stole that which is most invaluable – thousands of human lives. Here she is, cyclical history. As at the turn-of-the-century, and now, two decades before its end, wars have not achieved the goals they set out to attain. The goals of the Russo-Japanese and Afghanistan wars are, in principle, very similar. Their goals were the expansion of the sphere of influence of Russia, with a resultant decrease in the rate of development of unwanted (by the government) political processes inside the country . In 1904, Russia was in a revolutionary situation. "To hold off the revolution, we need a small, victorious war." said V.K. Pleve, the minister of internal affairs of the Czarist government. The opposition movement in the USSR was born in the latter half of the 1960's. By the end of the 1970's (as the Afghan war began), the movement was already developing in a few major directions, united under the struggle for democracy. The famous human rights defender, and "spiritual" father of Soviet dissidents, A.D.

Sakharov, while expressing opinions of the "sober-thinking" intelligentsia, called upon the government to withdraw its troops and let the United nations solve the problem. But the decision, made by the small Brezhnev-ruling elite, remained intact. You see, in the condition of the extreme arms race, the speedy establishment of socialism in Afghanistan, would confirm the idea of a pervasive world-socialism. This could significantly strengthen the position of the powers-that-be within the country and abroad. But a quick victory, as in the war with Japan, was out of reach. Instead, there was an activation of the democratic movement in the country, which, by the time of troop-withdrawal in 1989, gained a popular recognition. Of course the Afghan war was not the reason for the inception of perestroika, but it did serve as a background on which the existing contradictions of social and political life were clearly exposed.

Now Russia is going through a new crisis: the war in Chechnya, which is strikingly similar to the Afghan situation. The decision for the deployment of troops was made by a small group of officials and the president, with the consent of the parliament. As in 1979, the tactics and strategies of war, in particular those of street fighting, were not thought out. Instead of special forces, inexperienced recruits were sent into war. Even if the solution of the Chechen crisis were impossible to achieve without the involvement of the army, that involvement could at least have been organized along the best contemporary standards... Many, I think, will recall the "Desert Storm". The camera, mounted on a U.S. missile, shows an approaching Iraqi military warehouse, ... in a few seconds the picture disappears: the missile has exploded and the target is destroyed. And not a single American soldier dead. The Iraqi army is demoralized and left without means to fight back. Meanwhile our troops in Grozny are suffering casualties while trying to force Dudayev's fighters out of the Presidential palace. More forceful means cannot be applied: in the basement, (supposedly) there are hostages. But our soldiers have become hostages because of the incompetent actions of their leadership who sent first year draftees into this "meat grinder". On the whole, events in Chechnya give a very bad impression. Involuntarily one thinks that someone needed another "small, victorious war", one which once again turned out to be a failure. Experts think that this struggle with "banded-groups" might last for months, or could prolong, as the example of Ulster and Ireland has, for years. This war revealed the low battle-readiness of the Russian army: discord at the leadership level and the technical imperfection of the equipment. The global presence of Russia has been under-mined. "... And this is the army with which they have threatened us for so many years?... " is the statement that is reflective of the opinions of the Russian army, held by our former Western opponents, and of our enemies the world over. The army (and perhaps the space program) were the final entities Russia could brag about, in the faces of the countries of America and Europe, here at the doorstep of post-industrial civilization.

In reference to the existing crisis, some analysts notice the similarity of the situation before the putsch of 1991 and that of the present. Once again it can be said that "democratic trans-formations within the country are at a dead end". While these young soldiers in Chechnya cannot understand why they are sent to fight, many regular citizens also fail to understand the present state of affairs. The media often alters the facts. The dependency of the journalists on the financial support of commercial structures, their political biases, and also the willfulness of the bureaucracy who govern the media; all of these make the transition of information from their sources to the consumer somewhat difficult. Our modern information structures become less and less coherent to the public. The speech of the anchors seems to be purposely structured in such a way that highly educated people have a hard time understanding what it is that the person on the TV screen wants to say. The stubborn viewer, looking to make sense of the mysteries, switches from one channel to another and hears totally different explanations of known facts. In order not to be completely lost, a choice must be made of whom to trust. Thankfully, the choice is small: either RR, with its strong presidential bent and sometimes pretentious reporting on the opposition parties, or NT, sponsored by Most Bank, which transmits only to the central cities of Russia. How can we speak here about true democracy? Some newspaper articles have stated that we do not have democracy, but liberal anarchy. That is, without showing off, do what you will and you will not be held accountable later. Media ratings are on the rise because of the situation in Chechnya. And as a result, together with the reports from the front-line (in a time of peace), other events draw our attention as well. On the background of bloodshed the other "sores" of modern Russian society become more noticeable: criminal discord in politics, the economy, and the social realm.

Everyone has become involved in politics and economics, that is "those who had time to steal", in the words of a humorist/economist. There is a merger of economic and political capital in effect. And truly, it has long since occurred. Due to the lack of definite legislation, statesmen can allow the activity of some commercial structures, while exerting pressure on others. Of former Komsomol members, now called "New Russians", one sits on the chair of the city administration, another heads the joint-stock holdings. So, why not help out your former affiliates. And so the moneys, assigned for the unemployed, assigned to programs for creating new jobs, go into the hands of shrewd businessmen, and remain there. As a result, there is a separation in society of the very rich from the rest, who can only look on in envy at the lavish lives of the former. The psychological make-up of a Russian is such that envy often transforms into hate. "If a neighbor has two cows and I have one, it's better to poison one of theirs than get myself a second." Sounds familiar, does it not? This had better not be forgotten by those in power. Unfortunately, "the rest" have no influence over current affairs. Initiative belongs to the very rich. This was clearly shown during "Black Tuesday" when the ease with which one could destabilize the economy was demonstrated.

The "New Russians" are not anxious to invest in manufacturing, preferring rather to draw large profits in trading by means of "hidden" cheating of trusting citizens, who light-headedly bite on the bright commercials. Thusly (as in the case of Mavrodi[1]), by cheating countless Russians, one can become a hero/martyr by blaming all the misfortune on the government, and later become a legislator. Here "they" (the New Russians),

---

[1] A well-known financier, who was arrested when his mutual fund collapsed and subsequently escaped coniction by becoming an elected official

knowing the Russian psychology so well, take into account another well-known Russian feature: a certain admiration for cunning deception, respect for the mind and dexterity of the thief, resulting in a lenient reaction. Indeed Russians are not brought up on the principles of a law-governed state. So, what can be done?! The answer is simple: self-education. Only through self-education can society acquire the strength necessary to fight for law-guaranteed rights, human rights.

Right now our rights do not depend on us. It seems that the President is their guarantor, but the situation in which he finds himself gives reason for doubt. First, by his order, the artillery barrages the Russian Parliament, which was supposedly impeding reform. And not a single one of the central channels of information have uttered a word about whether or not this was a democratic measure. Then, his order to stop the bombing of Grozny went unheeded and the images, which proved the impotence of the presidential order, were broadcast to the entire world. What is left is only trust in one's self and faith. This is what Russians have always done. Throughout the whole of Russian history, the interests of the lower and most populous classes, the peasants and the workers, have been protected very weakly. Those who could break off from the common plight, could leave, if they were lucky, their mark on history. Such were the famous Russian gems: I. Fedorov, Yermak, the merchants Stroganoff, Minin, B. Khmelnitsky, S. Razin, S. Dezhnev, M. Lomonosov, Nikita Demidov, K. Bulavin, Pugachev, Polzunov, Kulibin, Bazhenov, M. Kazakov,

Argunovs[1] – all these people, who lived in the 17th and 18th centuries, left their mark. They all came from lower and middle class families. Those who could not, or chose not to, achieve their level, lived regular lives, despite the arguments of rulers, and the coming and going of czars. Life never stopped in the back country. She fed and clothed those fighting for power, while often suffering hunger and cold herself. This is how it is even now.

Slowly but surely, the manufacture of new products in the old Soviet factories is taking hold; the Kolhozes (collective farms) are beginning to sort out their problems. And if our government would seek the support of the simple folk from the provinces who have the ability and desire to work, then the country can be rescued from its industrial crisis. A healthy economy brings with it a healthy statehood. It has been that, with the flow of time, beginning with the first appearance of Slavic settlements, the bigger our country became, the greater the separation of the rulers from their people has grown. In Kiev's Russia the regular peasant addressed a noble as an equal. So what happened to us over ten thousand years of history? Why is the modern authority unreachable for the same peasant, but easily accessible for those of economic stature? It is we ourselves, proud of the great expanse of our country, who have

---

[1] Fedorov was a first Russian publisher, Yermak led the conquest of Siberia, the Stoganoffs were prominent merchants, Chmelnitsky was a Ukrainian leader who brought Ukraine into the Russian union, Razin was a famous Cossack rebel leader, Dezhnev was a famous explorer, Lomonosov was the father of Russian science, Demidov was a major industrialist in the Urals, Bulavin and Pugachev led peasant uprisings, Polzunov and Kulibin were inventors, Bazhenov, Kazakov and Argunovs were architects, --see Chronology for additional information.

placed power on such a high and unattainable pedestal from which we are so distant from its sight. All of this leads to a situation in which a small spark of freedom "at the bottom" immediately gives birth to the fire of hate toward those "at the top". This has happened a number of times in history. For example, in the 20th century: 1905, 1917, and the August putsch of 1991; and now it seems to be heading that way again. As a result, the government totally looses control of what is happening and falls from its great height. A holy place is never empty and is replaced by a new "king", who is the slickest of his competitors. To avoid this, to have government work for the good of the state and the people, power must become, foremost, "the region of responsibility". Fortunately, some have already come to understand this concept. However, if they seek power only for the sake of power, nothing will change: corruption, crime, growing unemployment, weak industry, and the disintegration of statehood.

I do not wish, in conclusion, to paint a dark picture of Russia. I, as well as all my great fellow citizens, believe in a better fate. Nor do I wish to build up cheerful hopes. History will sort it all out on its own. Whatever troubles Russia happens to be in, whatever moments of greatness, and in its moment of falling from its achieved height, the Russian peoples never lost their faith and always retained the sense of their uniqueness. And it is not only our oft-mentioned spirituality which is important here. It is simply that we have this national tradition; while being very skeptical of anything Russian, and considering foreign goods to be superior to our own, we, nevertheless, are painfully sensitive of our national reputation. We Russians are not satisfied with a premier global status, we need the world to recognize our unique role in the development of civilization. This thought is not new but precisely expresses my feelings – after all I am a citizen of Russia. Is it not this quality, of the Russian people, which will help us to regain our former pride in our fatherland, and find that certain path which needs to be followed. We still have a long way to go in climbing out of this "twilight region", which we have found ourselves in – hard, even, to say when it will occur. But, as is well-known, the twilight comes before the sunset, and before the sunrise as well. It is up to our choice and our actions, to determine whether the sun will rise over the Russian Empire, our whether the cold night will descend.

Tetelkin, Evgeny

A SEARCH FOR HOME IN THE TURMOIL OF RUSSIA

We lived in Tashkent, in the region of Tezinov, in Uzbekistan, commonly known as Tzinovka. Alexander Solzhenitsin mentions it in "First Circle".

We had a big house and a large yard where fruit trees and grapes grew, and tulips and peonies blossomed.

I liked Tashkent. The school where I studied was there. My friends lived there. A famous flea market, renowned in all of Tashkent, where I bought fish for my fish tank, was there.

Our family consisted of my mother, my grandpa – a disabled veteran of the war, my stepfather and my younger brother Arseny. There was a place for everyone in the big, comfortable house; even when my mother's older sister, my aunt, brought her two younger daughters to live with us. She herself lives in Petersburg (it was still called Leningrad back then), is a single mother of nine kids, and it is hard for her to support the entire family.

We lived a quiet and peaceful life until 1989. Then in Fergana, the pogroms of the Turk-Mesckh peoples began. My stepdad worked as a journalist for TASS in their Uzbek information bureau. He told us details which the local papers did not report. It was scary: arson, murder, torture...

170

Life suddenly and completely changed. Locals started treating us Russians very differently. We were told to "go back to your Russia!", or "soon we will start slaughtering you... " Gangs of Uzbek boys were blatantly roaming around threatening, insulting and sometimes beating boys of other nationalities. My mother and stepfather constantly warned me: "After school – straight home!" They tried to stop me from going into the city alone. I knew that at night my stepfather kept an axe by his side.

I saw that something terrible was happening, incomprehensible and unpleasant. My mother was nervous. Stepfather was often in a dark mood. They spent many nights on the porch, having long conversations about something.

Days passed and then months. Tension only grew. At school, the Uzbek language became the primary one. It had never been like that and even our teacher of Uzbek was easy on us. And all of a sudden: "Everyone must know Uzbek!"

For me all these slogans: "Sovereignty", "State Language" were empty sounds. However, in the city the signs in Russian started disappearing, all the bus, trolley, and subway stops were called out in Uzbek.

The adults in my family were saying more and more often that the children, that is Arseny and I, had no future in Uzbekistan. They started talking about Leningrad and moving there before it was too late. Grandpa said: "Go! Get settled and then I'll join you." It was sad to part with Tashkent.

My father wrote a critical article in which he touched on the financial interests of the big local bosses. After the article was printed he was called and told: "Now it's better for you to leave forever!" He said it was the third warning. He quit, we collected the necessary things and took a plane to Leningrad.

We arrived on the night of August 19. We stayed at my mother's sister's – our Aunt Tanya with all the children. She was happy to see us, because she had been urging us to come for a long time.

In the morning, when I awoke, I found out that there was a putsch going on in Russia. It turned out that the adults had been up all night listening to the local radio station, and a car, traveling up and down Moscow Prospect, the street our house faced, carrying a loudspeaker, had been broadcasting the message: "People of Leningrad, do not sleep! Men, come our to defend freedom! Everybody to Isakiev Square!"

Mother would not let my stepfather go. In the morning they went out together. Step father went to city hall and, using his TAAS identifications, spoke with someone from Mayor Sobchak's office and obtained copies of various documents, which turned out to be very useful to me four years later in preparing a presentation for one of my history classes.

They returned very excited, telling that Isakiev Square was surrounded by barricades, that there were big crowds at city hall, and that the building itself looked like a military headquarters: people armed with machine guns guarding the doors, orders being shouted, their faces tired and serious.

That night we listened to the radio again. They said the city was being approached by an armored column, but the military committee of Leningrad promised that the tanks would not enter the city. And then they reported that shooting started in Moscow, that there were casualties...

What was happening? Was this the Russia which we had longed to come to, to find peace and safety?

When finally the message came that the putsch failed and the putschists had been arrested, we had a celebration at Aunt Tanya's, with cake for the children and wine for the adults.

Two weeks passed. Mother and Stepfather got jobs at a local corporation. For two months we lived at Aunt Tanya's — fourteen people in three rooms. Then the firm moved us to apartments which it rented at Zhelyabov street.

What did I know about Russia while living in Tashkent? Probably only that which was included in the school curriculum: a bit of geography, a bit of literature, a bit of history... With the latter there were some problems. In the textbook I read one thing, but from the adults I heard something different, exactly opposite, and I, myself, saw something else. I saw a lot of homeless beggars everywhere (honestly, in Tashkent there are far fewer): old people, disabled, children... I saw a large number of drunks. I heard calls to : "Chase all the kikes and blacks with the dirty broom!" Turns out we left Uzbekistan to come to the same atmosphere; the only difference being that there Russians were being expelled and here they were doing the expelling. Of course everyone in Tashkent and Leningrad thinks that way. It is just that people are divided between smart and stupid, honest and dishonest, and honorable and despicable. There are many of the latter in Uzbekistan and in Russia. But, are there more of them than there are normal people? And if not, why are they allowed to get involved, get into my soul, spoil my mood and my life?... I don't understand!

Mother and Stepfather were making grandiose plans. Every morning they left to work, dropping Arseny at Aunt Tanya's, to be watched by the older daughters, and I was free to roam the city. Its history came alive to me. We lived in a good place for that: on one side – the river Moika and the house where Pushkin died after a duel; one the other, the Church of Spas, Mikhailovsky Park, Engineering Castle, Summer Garden.

I walked around and thought: "How could you name all the streets after the terrorists – Zhelyabov, Perovskaya, Halturin[1] (all these streets met at one intersection)? Of course they all were for the people, but if you think about it, they all are murderers. And we are told to honor their memory, be like they were. Why? Why did they tell us in school that Pavlik Morozov, who reported his father to the authorities, is a hero? Why did they not tell us to look up to Lermontov, Lomonosov, Akhmatova (poets, ed.)?... No!... we had to look up to the squealers and terrorists. So how come, then, do the intelligent people wring their hands and get surprised: "What a cynical youth we have, no ideals!" Where would they come from – ideals? First they said that Lenin and his group were the best people in the world. Now they say that they were the worst people in the world. It is easy to destroy monuments, but the new ones are not built. That's why everybody chooses his own. One looks up to Schwarzenegger, another to Bruce Lee, another to Viktor Tsoy[2].

---

1 Members of revolutionary party *Narodnaya Volya* (People's Will), who assasinated tsar Alexander II in 1881
2 A popular singer of late 1980-s

Soon, all of mother and stepfather's plans collapsed. The firm they worked at was constantly being restructured. In the end mother lost her job. Stepfather's salary was not enough to live on. The winter came. That's when I first saw long lines for bread.

Mother, Arseny and I, went back to Tashkent. Stepdad stayed behind in Leningrad. We lived apart for a year and a half.

In the summer of '93 we returned to St. Petersburg. Zhelyabov Street was renamed Konyushennaya, Halturin to Millionnaya, Peroskaya to Shvedsky Road. We were happy to be together again. We went for walks in Mihkailovsky Park and Summer Gardens.

Stepdad got another promotion. He was still working for the same company. However, when he became the chief editor, the firm stopped publishing books, and got involved in wood trade. He constantly went on business trips, staying for weeks at a time in places like Syktyvkar or Uhta. He would return tired and angry. He said that besides finding the wood, he also was working on returning money to the firm from the cheating suppliers. And in order to return the funds he had to deal with gangsters, who resolved all the issues faster than any court.

Unexpectedly we were contacted in St. Petersburg by a rich "sponsor" in Tashkent. He saw how we lived and offered to move us to Nyzhny Novgorod. He said that he had started a large and interesting business undertaking there, and that he needed trustworthy people – "his people". This "sponsor" promised that he would buy a condominium for us, for which

175

we would pay him back in installments. If it had been a stranger, we might not have trusted him. But this "sponsor" was almost a relative and therefore we agreed; especially in view of the fact that our lease in St.Petersburg was expiring.

We arrived in Nyzhny Novogorod on September 12, 1993. The "sponsor" took us directly from the station to a hotel. After a week it became clear that the condo purchase would have to wait.

October's putsch took place while we were still in the hotel. And again Mother and Stepfather were glued to the TV . And again there was fear and uncertainty.

And I thought: "When will it all end?" Is it true that Russia is a damned country? So much blood was spilled here. Is it not enough? They say that history teaches... but whom and what? It is clear that the second always want to become first, but cannot rise by humane means. And that is how kasha (porridge) starts to brew. Only *this* kasha is brewed on blood. This has always been the history of Russia. Take, for example, Kiev's Prince Svyatopolk I. He killed three of his brothers in order to attain their lands. When he was overthrown, he appealed to the Pechenegs (nomads) and the Poles for help. With foreign swords, he butchered his own Russian people. He had an appropriate knickname: Okoyannyi – "the one beyond redemption", and there have been many like him throughout Russian history. Look at Stalin! It is probably impossible to find another such beast in all of history.

And now another putsch. TV shows awful scenes: crowds of people in the streets butcher one another as if on Kulikov

Field [1] – But back then Russia was being defended from invaders. Now we fight amongst ourselves. And it is all because someone again wanted to reign supreme. It seems to me that if Russia cannot rid itself of this violent obsession with power, there will never be peaceful, stable life.

Then the TV reported good news: "Democracy has won!"

Mother and Stepfather, maybe seriously, maybe jokingly said: "Whenever we move, there is a rebellion in Russia!" This is why they decided not to leave Nyzhny Novgorod.

We lived in the hotel for two months, being moved from one room to another. Our "sponsor" suddenly disappeared and we never saw him again. Money was running out. Mother and Stepfather were consoling one another as best they could.

We managed to rent an apartment and move there. Stepfather works at a newspaper and writes children's books Mother is still not working. We pay forty dollars per month for the apartment and have two hundred thousand rubles (40 dollars) to live on (Grandpa has moved in with us).

Mother an Stepfather recently founded a club for the intelligentsia. One of the local deputies says that the city has no need for such a club, and mother and stepfather say that the city has no need for such a deputy. But the club will exist, it already does.

I do not know what "tomorrow" will be like. I hope it will be a happy one. And instead of news from the Chechen warzone, or yet another mafia-perpetrated crime, we will be told that the last homeless beggar has become a voluntary exhibit at the

---

[1] The site of a famous battle between the Russians and the Mongols in 1380.

177

Museum of History. And also, I would like us to have our own home. You know how good it is to have your own home.

Vasily Orlov and Victor Pavlenkov, May 15, 1995

Trubitsina, Irina

A DREAM OF RUSSIA

O my native country,
 great are your sufferings,
 but there is power unconquerable,
 and we are full of hope

N.P. Ogaryov

The path seemed unendingly long; all was submerged in the dark of night; only the path shone with a supernatural light. I knew not whether I was walking or flying along behind my companion. I do not remember how it was that I happened to be with him on the path. But we moved alone – without a doubt.

All of a sudden, a palace appeared before us . Upon entering, we found ourselves in a hall of striking grandeur. In its center was a lake, surrounded by flowers. Something attracted me, but I dared not ask about it.

Then three maidens arrived at the lake.

"We greet you, Yaissor.", they said. "What is the name of this newcomer?"

"Irina.", answered my companion, and turning to me said:

"These are my three sisters, Arechv, Yandoges, and Artvaza. Stay with them for awhile."

179

The maidens smiled and took me to the lake. Suddenly their faces became sad.

"Look what is happening in the world!" exclaimed Yandoges. "How evil has multiplied and how hatred has grown."

"They have always existed, but it was better... " uttered Arechv.

"Why ?" I asked.

"We see your times in the lake right now. The different countries of earth pass fleetingly before our eyes. People value their countries by mortal riches. The immortal ones they forget; they admire technological progress, but the environment is dying because of it. They see in everything only the external glare, but do not notice the true beauty and, what is more, they are destroying it... Look at Russia, your motherland." continued Yandoges. "What could you write about it?'

I started thinking. I recalled conversations about the generosity of the Russian people and the raging crime of our times, contemplation of the meaning of life and the search for happiness among the works of various writers... Involuntarily, I began reciting lines aloud:

> " O my dear Homeland,
> Land of so much suffering.
> O why do I love you,
> O my sad Russia?
>
> You are always choosing
> A way unknown to others.

There is a path in front of you,
But you will not follow others' footsteps.

When you see a flicker,
You are drawn to it.
But look! There is a fire,
But you don't notice it.

You rush about, my dear, from spark to spark.
But your people,
Shed tears,
Perish in lament.

'What are we to do? How are we to live?'
Questions pour down.
But to find the path,
is not very simple."

Scintillating radiance
Blinds the eyes.
How to understand which
Will lead out from darkness?"

"Enough." interrupted Yandoges. "You are asking a
question which has afforded many no peace."

"Yes." confirmed Arechv. "And you yourself can come
up with different versions. Gogol, as is well known, dreamt not
only of writing "Dead Souls", asking at the end of the first book:

"Russia, where are you racing to?"; but also resolved to answer the question in the following two books."

"And now, look into the lake." said Yandoges. "There you can see an excerpt of a composition by one of your contemporaries. Read it."

I heeded the advice. Small ripples on the water disappeared and the lines floated before my eyes:

"... In our era many paint Russia in such dismal colors, draw such pessimistic conclusions, that it seems there is no more unfortunate, deprived, pitiful, and ignorant country than she in the world. At first glance, these people are right. What makes up the history of our country? Constant mistakes and backwardness. Having crossed out the past, we have had an exulted and glorified motherland for seventy years, and believed in her happy future. Many did not know (or did not want to know) that people were dying in concentration camps, the atrocities which accompanied the revolution. Calling the revolution 'great", we all spoke of the deficiencies of yesterday's Russia: about serfdom, about the hardship of the people, and substantiated our words with the excerpts of the works of writers:

"... homeland.

Show me such a dwelling.
I have not seen a corner,
Where your sower and saviour,
Where the Russian peasant was not groaning?"

N. Nekrasov

"Russia, poor Russia... " (A. Blok)

When quoting Tyutchev, the usual example given was:

"These poor settlements,
  this meager nature –
  My land of long patience,
  The land of the Russian people!"

But further on, the poet spoke differently... Seventy years have passed...

Conversations arose about the total dilapidation and how everything 'required' immediate, even if violent, change. Now this big change has been in effect for a few years. And again, we only see its negative sides. Truly, yesterday's lives of our fathers and grandfathers turned out to be... mistaken. And, truly, vile and greedy instincts are becoming the standard, which in turn penetrate the society's subconscious and world outlook. Accordingly, society assumes its characteristic state. Our people have lost their national self-consciousness, their trust in themselves and the future; physically undermined by gigantic losses: the hunger of the past years, alcoholism.

But is it all that horrible in Russia? Did she not survive the Mongol-Tartar yoke, destroy it, and rebuild her strength a few centuries ago? She is being reborn today as well. Many people are starting to look differently at the world, returning to the wellsprings of the days of old. Look at how our temples are being reborn! Look at Russia with serenity. What does it lack for present and future grandeur? Immeasurable expanses were created to be the field of great events, experiments in civilized living; the multi-national make-up of the population can serve as a wellspring of different strengths and perfections; in the bowels of the earth there are unlimited riches. O Russia! "You will encompass all the climates; you hear within yourself all tongues; you find in your dwellings all levels of education; you embody the existence of the entire human race." Prophetically, Tyutchev said of you:

"He would not understand and would not notice
That proud foreign look,
That pierces and quietly shines
In your humble nakedness."

And I believe that my fatherland will yet shine and we will never agree with those who, through their logical conclusions, preach her demise. Let these people listen carefully to the words of the poet/prophet Tyutchev:

"By mind alone – not to be known,
By common yardstick – not to be gauged:
She has her own stately stature
In Russia one must only trust."

The water rippled again. Everything disappeared.

"What can you say about your Russia now?" asked Yandoges, turning to me.

"I do not know." I answered. "Of course Russia has a lot to be proud of. In the composition, the author makes no mention of many of the great people who lived in this country. How many scientists consider her to be their homeland... how many poets, writers! And the famous nobility, the military leaders: Alexander Nevsky, Dmitry Donskoy, A.V. Suvorov, P.I. Kutuzov, Zhukov... "Poor country"... And this poor country could stop the victorious march of Napoleon all by herself. This poor country, together with the Allies, conquered indomitable Hitler."

"That is right." interrupted Arechv. "But you do not see the spiritual beauty of yesterday's Russia... The names of the great heroes of piety, as for example Sergii Radonezhsky[1], whose influence on the destiny of Russia was invaluable, names well-known to many people. There is no country in the world so rich with beacons of faith as your homeland."

"People think that Russia does not remember, that it crosses out its history... That is wrong." continued Yandoges. "There exists a chronicle of the Russian kingdom. And, even during the Seventy Years of Communist rule, enemies could not destroy it. Visit the holy places of the fatherland: the historical memorials of fallen warriors, museums, monasteries, orthodox churches. Leaf through the calendar of church holidays and you will be convinced that there is no major event which has been left forgotten.

Today's Russia, despite all the difficulties and inner contradictions, is beautiful. Let us remember how the trees, in

---

[1] Russian saint who founded Holy Trinity Monastery and blessed Dimitry Donskoy for Kulikov Battle.

Spring, awake after a long sleep. They still look dead, but the sap is already flowing through their branches. A little time will pass and, as a green marquee, the trees will extend their branches. Such is Russia. Is it not true, Artvaza?"

"I cannot reveal, to a human, what tomorrow will bring." said the third maiden. "But I want to remind Irina of the prophecy which is known in her time: The land of Russia will be reddened with rivers of blood and much nobility will be destroyed for the great Emperor, and for the unity of his Reign; but God will not be angered indefinitely and will not allow the final destruction of Russia, because, in her alone, rest Pravoslavie (orthodoxy) and the remains of Christian piety. God will forgive Russia and bring her, through suffering, to great glory."

As Artvaza finished these words, Yiassor came up to me.

"It is time." said he.

O how I wished not to leave the maidens, but all disappeared in an instant... I again found myself back on the path with my companion.

"What did you talk about?" he asked.

"About Russia." I replied.

"And you did not guess whom you were so fortunate to speak with?"

"No, but they opened my eyes to a lot of things."

"That is true." said Yiassor. "If you want to reveal the secret of your experience, write our names down on paper, and read them attentively Please, do not forget what my sisters told you. Good-bye... "

Before I could reply, I found myself alone. Tears poured from my eyes, but my home waited for me... Russia waited for me.. There was nothing left but to return.

*Read backwards, Yaissor reads Rossiya (translate as Russia), Arechv reads Vchera (translates "yesterday"), Yandoges reads Segodnya (translates "today"), and Artvaza reads Zavtra (translates "tomorrow").

Tuhsanova, Elizaveta

VITYAZ AT THE CROSSROADS

The heavy, grey sky, merging somewhere in infinity with the steppes, weighed on Vityaz' shoulders as he towered, alone, over the feathergrass fields. Vityaz, at the crossroads, continued his eternal wandering through the land called Rus, or Rossiya.

From the very beginning it was unclear to him whether this land, which he had been sent to guard, was condemned to a murky fate, from creation, or whether it was through some fault of his own, a false choice of path. The ancient stone read: "To the left, you will loose your horse, to the right you will loose your head, straight on... "

In any case, Vityaz had become a symbol of this land.

Vityaz remembered how barbaric tribes of different origins and cultures had settled on the banks of full-flowing rivers and lakes.

Then, Rurik, the brave Viking, came to Rus, invited to Novgorod, and began to conquer lands to the south and to the east. They bent to his will and to the might of his Druzhina, his compatriot warriors. It was the beginning of Rus.

Vityaz remembered the crossroads on which destiny had brought him face to face with the Count of Kiev, Vladimir. Russia was already a state, but lacked one thing, a central faith to unite its people under a leader. Vladimir was faced with this choice of faith.

Later, his choice was explained in different ways. According to one version, Vladimir refused Catholicism, because it was too severe and the head of its church had too much power.

Islam was more to his liking. He liked religious fasting, its allowance for polygamy, but disliked its temperance doctrine. Byzantine Christianity allowed for only one wife, but permitted the drinking of spirits. So Vladimir baptized Rus in the Byzantine faith.

Of course this legend is not completely true, but we do know that, a millennium ago, Vladimir chose a path between East and West. And for the centuries to come, determined the ways of the nation.

He left the crossroads having given the people a single god, which unified the various tribes, while strengthening his power over the people. Faith helped in difficult times, brought people together in the face of disaster, and led them into battle. In the darkest hour, Sergii Radonezhsky appeared in Russia and dedicated his life to unifying the various dukedoms around the central Muscovite principality. He blessed Dmitry Donskoy on the fields of the battle of Kulikov. Who knows if, without this single faith, Russia would have been able to survive the Tartar-Mongol yoke, and stand as a buffer between wild Asia and developing Europe for three hundred years...Vityaz recalled how, half a century later, the monk of Troitsk-Sergeev Lavra, painted his Holy Trinity in memory of the great zealot, Radonezhsky. During this era, the united state was again bled by inner wars, and, as if in prayer for Russia, Rublev wrote his *Three Angels*, who symbolized the indomitable holy Trinity – unifying and uplifting Russia. This was the first icon in which angels became more humane and compassionate, as opposed to the cold, stern Byzantine holy men.

In the history of any state there are bloody episodes. But there are not too many lands in which so much blood has been shed. Perhaps it all started with the baptism by "fire and sword"?

These were not only battles with invaders. There was also constant inner strife, such as that suffered at the hands of Ivan "the Terrible", and his Oprichnina (secret police), even the blood of his own son stained the hands of this "Bloody Czar". Nevertheless it was during his reign that Russia was also strengthened and enlarged. Kazan and Astrakhan came under his rule. The whole series of pseudo-czars began with his murder, in Uglich, of the young prince Dmitry: Gregory Otrepyev, pseudo-Dmitry II, later followed by Razin, Pugachev, and the Countess Tarakanova...crossroads, crossroads... Vityaz had crossed so many of them, following the whims of bloody self-appointed leaders and power mongers! ...Peter I had little chance of becoming Czar. He was the fourteenth child of the Czar Aleksey Mikhailovich. Nevertheless, it was the fate of Russia to be ruled by this man.

It was a rare, and perhaps unique, case when Russia moved from the dead point and took the path oriented to the West. Peter chose that road and went down it, destroying everything in his path. In an unbelievably short period, he built a navy and strengthened the army. He allowed for upward mobility.

Russia achieved an access to the sea, the youth attended European universities, and beautiful St. Petersburg arose from the swamps. That headlong push required many sacrifices, which nobody cared to count.

Vityaz fell into deep thought: perhaps all those people had accepted their deaths in the swamps as an unavoidable fate. The strong hand was always loved in Russia, they even mourned the death of Ivan the Terrible. Not all, of course, but many. Even the writers said: "The more sternly a noble rules, the more acceptable it is to the peasants."

In one way or another, the 18th century was an epoch of progress. Mid-century, a German princess seized the power from her husband, and became known in history as Catherine the Great. The educated queen corresponded with Voltaire. Under her rule science flourished and Russia moved closer to European culture. Here they are, Catherine's grandees rendered by the Russian portraitists Rokotov, Levitsky, and Borovikovsky: powdered wigs, clean faces, reddened, smiling lips. It is impossible to imagine that these are the children of the bearded Boyars, dressed in their unseemly Medieval garb.

The 19th century, later to be known as "golden", saw an abundance of sharp minds and great talents. These people had a tendency towards monologues, which is why they had such difficulty hearing one another:

Monologue of Lishny Chelovek[1]

"At the turn of the century, after our victory over Napoleon and triumphant return from Europe, I realized how much we had fallen behind.

I tried to explain it all in the Salons, I spoke of the necessity for reform, of progress, trying to explain that serfdom had lost its place and was slowing us down on our way to prosperity. How inspirationally I spoke! How I believed I could make a difference!

Pushkin failed to understand why I "cast pearls before swine". Griboedov, who described me under the name of Chatsky, had somewhat shared my sentiments and made me an unlikely hero/lover of classic comedy.

I admit, I was not always right. I wished for good for my people, but I did not know that, and had not counted on their help.

Later we, people of the same convictions, united. O God, what a utopia it was! We were noble to the degree of self-sacrifice. We were prepared to compromise our own interests, to refuse our privileges, but when we gathered on Senate Square, in December[2], all we could do was kill Miloradovich, and later be hanged and exiled. But we did it in the name of our

---

[1] Literary character, present throughout 19th century Russian literature, exemplifying a disenchanted, educated member of the intelligentsia, who cannot apply his talents and energy within the existing social order.
[2] The Decembrist Uprising, was a failed uprising by the civilian and military Russian intellectual elite, opposing the coronation of Nicolai I. Miloradovich was the general governor of St.Petersburg. The ensuing reign of Nicolai I was marked by the reactionary policies of his Interior Minister, Arakcheev.

fatherland, which had gone down a dead end and was staggering in its development under the rule of Arakcheev.

Then I became bored. I had not realized myself. Nikolai I's painful reaction had begun. I had a lot of useless knowledge and all the struggles of my soul were spent either in duels and meaningless endeavors, like Pechorin[1], or had wilted under the weight of the knowledge that I had grown old, like Eugene Onegin[2]. I circulated in court life and found no goals to pursue. Everything at court was foreign to me, and I was foreign to it. I was an idle talker, like Rudin[3], content that, at the end of my time, I was able to make a contribution.

I gradually changed and became the nihilist, Bazarov[4]. I wanted to change something, but could only destroy, not thinking of the consequences... I thought of myself as Napoleon and to check that idea, I killed the old moneylending woman. When I became an angel, they called me an idiot.[5]

I wavered between the Slavophiles and the Westernizes. They all were right in some way; the former in their claim that Russia was not the West, and that all that flourished in Europe could not be transplanted to Russian soil; the latter were right in their claim that we should not isolate ourselves from the West.

Meanwhile, Russia remained agrarian. The medieval traditions persisted and the economy stagnated, only beginning to develop at the end of the century. As an answer to the growing social contradictions, absolutism was strengthening, and the

---

[1] Character in M. Lermontov's novel, *Hero of Our Times*.
[2] Character in A. Pushkin's novel, *Eugene Onegin*.
[3] Character in Turgenev's novel, *Rudin*.
[4] Character in Turgenev's novel, *Fathers and Sons*.
[5] References to Dostoevsky's novels, *Crime and Punishment* and *The Idiot*.

abominable bureaucracy spread its long arms everywhere, dividing people into the "fourteen ranks". People served, not the country, but those who were just a rank above them.

Yes, my century is a paradoxical one, but a golden one. Remember all of those who made it so: Pushkin, Lermontov, Gogol, and Dostoevsky... Why do I name them? You know them all anyway... those great creators, whose works grace the Tretyakov Gallery and the Russian Museum... Glinka, Mussorgsky, Tchaikovsky, and the Temple of Christ the Savior... I painfully searched out the way, but I did not unite with my epoch, because I lost my roots with the people... "

The 19th underlined two eternal Russian questions: "What to do?", and "Who is guilty?", but did not resolve them.

At the beginning of the next century, a poetry flourished which would later be called decadent. The start of reforms promised prosperity... It was an impetus theretofore unknown. In just a decade Russia left a half-feudal existence, and quickly approached a European standard. The industry underwent rapid development. Foreign investment poured in, thanks to statesmen and entrepreneurs. Gradually, but steadily, the agrarian question was being resolved.

But... the people were forgotten. Abandoned, they lost faith in their rulers, which is ruinous for Russia. First, they followed Gapon, who led them to the imperial palace on January

9,1905.[1] Later, the social revolutionaries and Bolsheviks appeared; they needed to be led by someone. The simple workers more easily understood the Bolsheviks, who called for the dictatorship of the proletariat. They also turned out to be the more expedient movement.

Crossroads... 1917. Russia takes a sharp turn. To where? Socialism. Was it the socialism which Chernyshevsky dreamt of?[2] Was it towards the ideal of Tomaso Campanella, the City of the Sun? Did the way to that beautiful city have to be through the blood of civil war, the destruction of faith, which had strengthened Russia in the days of trial. Nevertheless, people went that way, following someone's will and strong arm.

In their incomprehensible fanaticism, they destroyed the temples built by their ancestors. But why should this be so incomprehensible? Fanaticism and religion share a doubtless, dogmatic faith.

Vityaz recalls the frenzied "arch-priest"[3] and his followers: Boyarynya Morozova, with her shining eyes, crossing herself with two fingers, the Countess Urusova (the spiritual daughter of Avvakum), and those, who, in the name of the old faith, burned themselves as families, even entire villages, despite the fact that their new faith was not much different. He remembered those who left for far away lands, so they would not have to cross themselves with the "devilish pinch". Without thought or

---

[1] "Bloody Sunday" was a massacre of petitioners in St. Petersburg by Czarist troops, which eventually led to the first Russian revolution.
[2] As rendered in his novel *What is to be done?*, which became a major literary work and political treatise for the 19th Russian intelligentsia.
[3] Reference to monk Avvakum, a spiritual leader of Old Believers

doubt, they died for the purity of the faith, and their descendants, with equal wantonness, tore down the temples.

These post-revolutionary times are remembered differently by different people. Some remembered the great enthusiasm of the greatest construction projects of all time, Magnitka[1] and Dneproges[2]. Others remember the dead-ends of Lubyanka[3] and the Gulags. Bunin and Shalyapin[4] died in exile. Esenin and Mayakovsky[5] committed suicide... perhaps in Russia. Rachmaninov composed his music in America. The academician Vavilov[6] was condemned an enemy. There were a lot of "enemies" among the doctors, writers, and scientists.

——————

"Grandfather, why do they call this place the glade of Arsen?"

"There used to be a man, Arseny, who clear-cut the woods in this here Taiga, plowed the land, and built the road to the village. He cultivated wheat in this region."

"... And where is the glade now?"

"It has been overgrown again... in taiga (woods) everything becomes overgrown."

"Why?"

[1] Major iron ore mining field established the Bolchevik government.

[2] Hydroelectric dam on the Dnepr.

[3] Headquarters and infamous prison of the Communist secret police.

[4] Bunin was a Nobel Prize winner of literature. Shalyapin was a famous opera bass.

[5] Great Russian poets.

[6] Major Russian scientist whose research in genetics was proclaimed the "bourgeois science of Western imperialism".

"He was declared a Kulak[1]."

Uncertain times... A Nobel Prize[2] writer is exiled from his homeland. An academician is awarded the "Hero of Labor"[3], and is another Nobel winner, in internal exile in his own country...

Vityaz had shook off the memories of his millennia-long wanderings. It seems that another set of crossroads had been passed. What lies beneath his feet... a hard road, or more treacherous terrain? He looks around. Again, a tricolor flag, and, again, banners are being raised over the cupolas... Again the Slavophiles and Westerners, Democrats and Monarchists, even people with swastikas on their sleeves...Has it not been a mere half-century, since these people exerted all their strength to destroy German fascism, paying no mind to the dire price that had to be paid. Vityaz still remembers that day in May: there was jubilation and many a teary eye.

On the streets of the formerly "closed" city, foreign speech is heard. Here is another sign of new times: multitudes of laryok (small convenience booths). One can study history in their windows: Vodkas of Peter I, Alexander II, Lev Tolstoy, Rasputin, and Yeltsin...

---

[1] A farmer accused of being a "class enemy" for refusing to join the process of collectivization.
[2] Alexander Solzenitsyn.
[3] Andrei Sakharov.

But the people, it seems, have been forgotten once again. They are loosing their trust in their leaders. They are confused by much of what is going on around them. Vityaz, himself, is unclear about many things. He cannot even tell where Russia ends these days. For example, Chechnya, ... is it Russia?

Yes, it is hard to sort out what is going on today in Russia and, what is most important, is... what lies underfoot... road or swamp?

Vityaz squints his eyes to see further, beyond the horizon, to grasp what lies ahead. But he can only make out a large stone marking yet another crossroads on the endless steppe, which merges with the cold, grey sky.

Holina, Kseniya

THE SPIRITUAL QUEST OF GREAT RUSSIA

Many books have been written about Russia's past, present, and future by scientists, philosophers, writers, and poets. The variety of their points of view were influenced by the rich historical complexities of the country and by German, French, and English cultural influences over the centuries, as well as by the contemporary epoch, which is very important, since there are few authors who were truly independent. It is not my right to judge one or another vision of the life of our state. But within certain limits I can express my opinions on the posed question and will therein draw on the beautiful book by Daniil Andreev, "Rose of the World". While I doubt that my views will seem traditional, these are my impressions of Russia; Russia as one of the creative entities of the world.

Russian culture, as well as the Russian state, came into being much later than many other world cultures. At the time of its inception, around the 8th and 9th centuries A.D., other ancient civilizations, such as the Egyptian and Greco-Roman, had already passed the zeniths of their existence and were in decline. They gave humanity beautiful sons and daughters, enriched the treasuries of art with masterpieces; then stagnating and unable to develop further, were giving way to other cultures. Byzantium has a very special place amongst civilizations (we touch upon it since it is directly connected to the destiny of Russia). While other states had the chance for further development, Byzantium ceased to exist soon after the period which we are about to describe.

The borders of young Russia touched the Byzantine Empire, which was the only large concentration of Orthodoxy, and therefore embodied the last chance for the Church to be a partner of the State, and not the head of secular power, such as Catholicism was at the time. And so Russia inherited the spiritual experience of Byzantium, and its unfulfilled goals. Therefore, as historians would say, Russia came under the influence of the Byzantine tradition: "The Christian mythology flowed powerfully into the people's consciousness, charming their hearts with the images of the Almighty Virgin and Holy Men, which rose to the heights of holiness, up from the darkness of Judaism and Byzantium. From the holy places of Jerusalem and Afon, from the cupolas of Tsargrad, shone white rays, warming the soul and joining it to the glory of Orthodox creativity: monk's deeds, following the ways of the holy men, spiritual elation, meekness, church building, fasting. There came as well a warning: "Tremble in fear before God's wrath..." This "trembling fear" brought with it asceticism into the developing Russian church and the prevailing conviction: "The world lies in evil."

But Christianity did not come to an atheistic Russia. There was a pre-existing mythology, which, while not yet mature, was a reflection of man's love of natural wonders, it was reflected as well in everyday events, the family, and the defense of the country against marauding nomads from the steppes. It would seem that Byzantine Christianity, being the mature religion, which flowed powerfully into Slavic paganism, would have destroyed these incomplete sets of beliefs. In reality this did not happen. Dense woods, full rivers, and unlimited fields insured "the connection of humanity with the forces of nature", and saved one's appreciation of life and the creative approach to work. The mythology of ancient Russia retreated into the lower classes and was most reflected in everyday life: "Grass patterns on textiles and window frames were far removed, in their purity, from Christian ideals, as was the firebird of our fairytales, the heroes of Russian folklore, the architectural particularities of our buildings, and stylized roosters and fantastic animals enriching the stoves and roofs of our houses.

"This is how the foundations of a dual-faith were laid down"; one which did not disappear from Russia until the 20th century. Christianity and ancient Slavic sets of beliefs coexisted in parallel, never merging, instead supplementing one another amongst the folk, in doing so, created a harmonious union.

We considered the formation of Russian culture and life-perception, but forgot to mention one super-important fact which would later influence the life of the country as a whole. Russia's future role in the world consists not of carrying the burden of the Byzantine legacy, but that of fulfilling its own exceptional task. The essence of this task consists of the following: to climb to the highest level of development, in order to lead other cultures and peoples. "From the beginning, the Christian myth gave a premonition of this world-mission to the consciousness of Russian folk – not a mission of global imperial power, but a mission of a highest truth of sorts, one which must be declared and established on earth for the good of all. This is substantiated by the tone of Kiev's and Moscow's chronicles and in the naive, but unquestionable ideals of Bylina (Russian traditional heroic poem), which thought of their heroes as messengers of and fighters for a highest truth, which shines to all those open to it. Further, this consciousness-of-self created the ideal image of Holy Russia: not only great, powerful, and beautiful, but indeed holy; finally, in the idea of a Third Rome this ideal is crystallized absolutely." All of this is to happen over many centuries; and the essence of the task will be further explained. Now we will examine the history of the state, and how it proceeds towards its most-important goal.

Russia has overcome many obstacles. These have left deep traces in its destiny, and will strongly influence its future. The young Russian nation has gained by experience and learned through mistakes. Many were costly mistakes and we missed many an opportunity to further develop our consciousness!

The first major cataclysm for the country was the Tartar-Mongol yoke. The Russian people found themselves ruled by ignorant tribes who, unsatisfied with their tribute, periodically destroyed and robbed the cities and country settlements, which were the centers of culture and religion. In addition to this, Russia was in a state of feudal fragmentation. She was unable to free herself from the hated yoke through the independent, unaligned forces of her various counties. Thusly, the idea of unification was born.

Any state is far from an ideal form of social organization. It always carries within itself a grain of forceful subjugation. But, to this day, humanity has not found a more perfect system of micro-organization. What can we say of the 14th and 15th centuries, when the state was the only plausible method of freeing Russia from Mongol dominance? Russian peoples had not yet had the ability to think in perspective. Before them stood the choices of total annihilation, or a centralization of the power in the hands of one specific county, that is, the creation of a state, which later, without a doubt, would turn against its own people. Russia chose the latter.

The country became a unified and mighty monolith, able to repel any external enemy. The heads of this monolith, prior to Ivan IV, "The Terrible", were the great counts of Muscovy, who drew most of their support from the "nobility and freemen" (Pushkarev).

It is important to note the fact that, until the latter half of the 16th century "historical experience had not put Russian consciousness in contact with the unsolvable contradictions of thought and spirit", that is, during this time great thinkers were not being born, in the full sense of the term. "The Tartar struggle was a struggle with a concrete, and clearly defined, enemy of the entire nation: such a struggle could only further the development of a whole, rock-solid national character". Remember, for example, Alexander Nevsky, Dmitry Donskoy, Andrey Rublev, and the author of "A Word on Igor's Regiment". The situation was radically changed by the epoch of the rule of Ivan IV and the Great Sedition which ensued. Being called on to perform the role of an implementor of reform, which should have prepared Russia for the transformations of Peter the Great, this first Russian Czar (Ivan IV), did not only fail to fulfill the task set before him, but became a tyrant, who spread fear into many hearts, and began the destruction of the statehood. His legacy was continued by Pseudo-Dmitry I and Vasily Shuisky. The Great Sedition made even clearer to the people the "unheard-of crimes committed, without punishment, by heads of state; their spiritual tragedies, shown to all; the conflicts of their consciousness; their petrifying fear of having to atone for their sins; the ephemeral nature of the czar's statue; the fragility of all of the beginnings of reform, which seemed not to be blessed from above; mass visions of light and dark warriors, fighting one another over something deep-rooted, untouchable and holy in people, perhaps a God-like entity" People were beginning to sense, not a clearly-apparent enemy, but elusive and undefined dark forces, emanating from God's appointed ruler, the Czar.

So why did the Russians have to go through so much suffering? Russian culture and the consciousness of its people, before the described tribulations, were in a state of prolonged adolescence (more than 800 years). As described earlier, the country was not producing thinkers: there was a wholeness in people's characters, external contradictions did not exist at all; this is why thoughts of good and evil did not exist. Ivan "The Terrible" and the Great Sedition made the separation of these two opposites very unclear and fluctuating. They forced Russians to consider these issues.

On one hand, they were a people who were "very naive, spiritually; and very weakened of soul, under the Tartar yoke", and, on the other, Europeanism was about to flood into Russia in the wake of Peter's reforms. Under such circumstances, the more mature Western culture would have strangled Russian spirituality, the sprouts of her originality, – that is, all that was the foundation, the "one and only role of the Russia's mission in the world". The country was saved from all of this by the horrific experience it underwent during the "dynastic interregnum". The Great Sedition led the people out of the state of childhood. A transformation from "cultural adolescence, to young adulthood".

Thus was the epoch of Peter the Great.

This period in the life of the state was truly an epoch; an upheaval in consciousness took place in many people. Russia, having spent so many centuries "boiling in its own juices" and jealously defending its originality simply had to open itself to other countries and cultures to carry out its great mission. This became the main goal of Peter the Great. The country had to appear in the international arena, not as a backward, barbarian tribe, but as a great empire, carrying with it colossal potential. Peter, a genius in the art of statesmanship, understood this need, and finally achieved its end by "chopping a window to Europe". This is how Western civilization gushed into the consciousness of Russians. Of course, one cannot really consider a process of joining world culture to be a blessing falling on the head of the Orthodox Russian (pravoslavnyi). It was far from this, it was all very painful and complicated. However, through the experience, Russians were able to see and understand the lives of others, and acquire further life-experience, from which Russia, at the time, was quite distant (not in a spiritual sense, but in an economic and social one).

To carry out the given task, reform had to be implemented in order to prepare the country for these decisive steps. Needed, first of all, was "the abolition of the boyars (the old nobility), as a ruling sect unable to perform at a level of historical magnitude, and the transfer of the leadership to the dvoryanstvo (new nobility) and the middle class. And why was there no power transferred to the clergy and the peasantry? The clergy was unsuited because their leadership within the state would have brought Russia into a situation similar to that of the catholic nations of the Dark Ages. And the peasantry was the most backward of all the social classes. It was still in need of help and, first of all, had to be liberated from serfdom.

Then came the epoch of Peter, a seething epoch of the construction of the new and the destruction of the old, which reflected in the customs and traditions of everyday life of Russians, the epoch of the expansion of Russian consciousness, came to an end. What sort of legacy did all of this leave us with? "The window to Europe was chopped through." – that was without question. The boyars had been abolished as the leading force, and dvoryanstvo took its place. But the middle class had not received its well-deserved role in the state and the peasantry was entirely forgotten. Large-scale reform was not attained. As deep as Peter dug his spade into the virgin soil, he still could not get to the root. But that was only half of the tragedy; the available time had not yet elapsed. The real tragedy consisted of the fact that those who followed did not want to act for the next 150 years. Such inactivity of the rulers, which governed the country after Peter, would show its ruinous effects much later. I do not want to go into the details of all of their lives, but wish only to point out consequences which were the cause of the establishment of the ugly, socialist regime at the beginning of the 20th century.

The first consequence was economic and cultural. It is no secret to anyone that a majority of the population consisted of the peasantry (80%). Besides being the largest sector, it was also the poorest. The middle class also had not developed to the necessary degree, and was therefore not in a good situation. How can one expect a country to grow under such conditions? The second consequence was moral-psychological: "that is, the habits of a slavish mentality were firmly and deeply-ingrained in the psychology of the masses: a lack of the complexities of civil feelings and ideas, a degrading submissiveness, disrespect for individuality, and, finally, the propensity to become a despot, should fate raise the slave out of his usual state of existence.

The third consequence was religious. It grew out of the first two: "you cannot sit down with only luchina (kindling), malnourished, unenriched by any book, with hungry children, and create "spiritual genius"." Without these conditions, the regime which appeared in our state in the 20th century would not have been possible. It simply could not have existed without people "trained to suffer all deprivation, mediocrity, and poverty", without a slavish mentality, or without the enslavement of his spiritual, creative thought. Indeed, Russia was hereby delayed in carrying out its true historic mission for an undetermined period of time.

Since we touched upon the theme of a highest goal for Russia, let us now discuss the original source – the Orthodox Christian church. We already noted a major positive significance for the country, which was embodied in the decision of the holy Count Vladimir on state religion. The significance was that Orthodoxy, given to us by Byzantium, was devoid of the thirst for power seen so strongly in Catholicism, Islam, and Judaism. Originally the Russian Church was the spiritual partner of the state, later, it turned into its supporter; further on, we will see how it gradually lost its great role.

Ivan the Terrible created in Alexander Sloboda (a settlement exempted from normal obligations) a "devilish charicature of the monastery", poorly understanding the true meaning of its creation. The Great Sedition followed hereafter, making the lines between good and evil uncertain, obscured, and fluctuating. "As a result of the experience of these years, there came into existence a common attitude amongst the people – one which, in its logical development, led to the great Raskol (Great Church Divide)". Herein we can already see the foundation being laid for the huge differences in the world views of different classes of people. The situation was worsened, and became an impetus to the Raskol, by the attempts of the patriarch Nikon to subjugate the Czar's authority to his own. Such a change in the position of the Russian Church, which was never a power monger, would have put enormous, horrific, incomprehensible, and therefore impossible demands on the Church: the theocratic attempts of Nikon were cut short, but there remained in the soul of all an awful fear of evil, which made its nest in the holiest place for Russians, that is, in the church. Thusly it came to the Raskol, which divided the spiritual forces of our people. The church was further reduced by the reforms of Peter I. It was assigned a small corner of the great state, which turned it into a servant.

"As sad as such a degradation of the Church, in its submission to the state, is... from the religious, cultural, and Orthodox-confessional points of view, it is still the lesser of two evils, when compared with the opposite extreme."

All in this world is interrelated, everything flows from one thing to the next. Such was the case of the regime which came to dominate the country at the beginning of the 20th century. It was nothing but a consequence of the neglect of those who followed Peter and the servitude in which the Church found itself.

It is well-known that in the middle of the 19th century, in western Europe, a "universal doctrine" was formed, which was later named Marxism-Leninism. It is important to note the inner contradiction of the doctrine, the great gulf between its methods and its ideals. We all know the great ideas of universal equality and brotherhood, but, in this case, the way to their implementation was through military struggle, violent take-over of power, the merciless murder of enemies, and the dictatorship of one class (really only of its elite). The economic side of this doctrine, "theoretically well-established and morally justified", underwent serious distortions, because of the aforementioned gulf, just as its implementation came about. The philosophy of the doctrine was founded on the principles of the secular era (into which western countries had already entered) and therefore was shallow in its rationale, and devoid of spirituality and God's grace.

Due to the causes described above, this doctrine found fertile ground in Russia and began to develop. It had not been long since the positive ideals of this movement had won a place in the dreams of many people. The tasks of global fraternity, which were placed before Russia, had seemingly begun their implementation. That much deeper, then, was the disenchantment when it turned out that the regime had been used for the will of a terrible tyrant.

Stalinist Russia was another epoch in the lives of the Russian people; one of terror, blood, and godlessness. There is no need to state in detail what Russia turned into, as far as economics and social issues are concerned, nor reiterate the effects which strengthened the slave mentality of millions, nor need we mention the paralysis of any fresh thought, or the collapse of spirituality and religion. Russia had come into contact with something thus-far unknown in the history of mankind; if one examines the tyrannies of other eras, there is little chance one could find any to compare with that of Stalinism. But all of this was a valuable experience as well: even though it was horrible and painful, and it would have been better had it never happened, having gone through it, the Russian people will strive to prevent a recurrence of this great evil.

We comprehend events more clearly when they become parts of history (one can see things more clearly from a distance than up close). This is why it is difficult to give an assessment of current events. I shall not go into the description of reforms, the economic state of this society, the actions of politicians – all of these will be a rich field of activity for our descendants who will analyze our mistakes, as well as the correct actions taken. Instead I will write about my vision of the important aspects of the moral issues facing society.

Russia is currently going through a very complex period. She is at a fork in the road and the destinies of the peoples who comprise the state, and that of the rest of the world, depend on the choice she makes.

The most terrible legacy inherited from Stalinism is the spiritual impoverishment of the people. Over a few decades, the authorities methodically beat the ideas of God and a higher morality (which were preached by the Church) out of the consciousness of people. A gaping emptiness remained in place of that which was occupied by the Church.

Why lose such a well-tested lever for the manipulation of the masses?... A cult of "the leader" – "the father of the people" was created, and simultaneously raised, on an empty pedestal, a thoroughly materialistic science, which killed any spirituality with its logical deductions. Nobody noticed this, until now. It was hidden under the piles of the dead bodies of true scientists who worked selflessly for the good of the people and did not claim such high positions. In the consciousness of the people, science became a God-like entity, capable of providing everything. To this day, society has not freed itself from such calculating atheism.

Religion in Russia has not died, it is still smoldering in an unfortunately small number of souls. There was a need for a fresh breath from the winds of change to make the fire burn and light the hearts of people who have been in a state of spiritual paralysis for many years. This happened around 1985. I could be doubted on this, but people suddenly felt a need for something supernatural, hidden until now behind "seven seals", a need for religion. In our search and need for the seed of truth, we take up astrology, palmistry, witchcraft, and faith healing, but still fail in our attempts. However, through the gradual process of trial and error we can approach that which is real. I believe that the recent laying of the foundation of the Church of Christ the Savior in Moscow was symbolic of such a spiritual quest.

Temples in Russia were always held in high esteem during times of trouble. This is how people expressed their strong faith and hope, hope for help from above, in their aspirations towards purity, and in their attempts to overcome difficult circumstances. Today, again, as many centuries ago, we are searching for this tranquillity and hope. Our only hope consists in the notion that the Church reemerge as it was in the past. We live in a transient world, life does not proceed without change. Why should we not apply this notion to religion as well?

Let us turn to the other side of our common consciousness. For Russians the window to Europe and America is once again open and we can once again embrace the more progressive legacies of other countries, using the opportunity to rebuild our state. First, however, that which we adopt from Western culture are not at all its best aspects and, secondly, we are attempting to recreate our society in the image of another society which is foreign to us. Russians are forgetting that every nation has its own inimitable ways, that their homeland is unique and, who knows, perhaps we have even been called upon to implement a principally new social order.

One more important fact must be mentioned: the break-up of the Soviet Union, the dissolution of a great empire. Russian eastward expansion began at the end of the 16th century. What were the reasons for this process? Why did our people, so thinly spread out over the mostly uninhabited eastern European plain, in a brief hundred years, through efforts, not of the state, but by private individuals, take over a space which is three times larger than the territories of their homeland; a cold, stern, and uninhabited realm, rich only in fur and fish, and in the following century even move to cross the Bering Strait, reaching all the way to California? Many will cite economic motivations (i.e. fur, fish). Would it not have made sense to stop at the Urals and Western Siberia which could have supported a Russian population ten times larger than the numbers of Cossacks who initially crossed this "rock belt" (Urals); why, then, had China, which was much closer to these territories, not annexed them. They say that the serfs were running away from the power of their masters, but was it not possible for them to settle in Ob', Irtish, or Angara, where they would have been without noble masters? Instead, however, they went into the wilderness, across gigantic rivers and into the impenetrable Taiga (virgin forests of Siberia); through regions populated by other tribes who gave resistance, and finally reaching the Pacific, even made the passing to North America. What are the reasons behind this migration? From the depths of the centuries, there arose a vague understanding of Russia's global mission. Russia was destined to fill the gap between all cultures by coming into direct contact with them, making it possible, a few centuries later, to deliver that highest truth for which this great country was created.

And now peoples, who for years have been considered our brothers, have started living independent lives. Perhaps this is not such an terrible occurrence, but evil does lie in the civil strife, which further destabilizes already weak societies.

Living in an epoch of astonishing change, I noticed a paradox in the moral state of the Russian people. Some (who are unfortunately a minority for now) are striving for the highest spirituality, conscious of the fact that it is in the immediate moment that one must act, work, create, without a moment lost; meanwhile others put off carrying out the direct tasks until tomorrow saying: "first I must own this or the other thing, then I will begin to create spiritual values". There is yet another category of people who are concerned only with the accumulation of material goods. Most likely, insufficient time has passed for these individuals to recognize the necessity for changes on a different level. Worse even, to me, is the inaction of those who understand the situation. It need not be that this analysis apply only to the state of spiritual affairs.

Indeed, life is not sweet for Russia right now. But which nation has not experienced such phases of "interregnum", unsettledness, and change? I am sure that our country will avoid this dead-end, since everything passes in time. The important thing is to act, to create in the present, for a brighter future.

Russia's tomorrow is closely tied to its today and its yesterday. Her future will be determined by which path she chooses. It is not my intention to paint a picture of gloom, so let us imagine, then, what awaits if Russia does choose a spiritual path of development.

In this essay, Russia's unique task has been mentioned repeatedly. It is a great and difficult task. This is why a powerful empire such as ours is called upon to carry it out. It is still a commonly held opinion that the achievements of material gain will necessarily be followed by spirituality. Why, then, have the countries of the western world failed to reach the high spirituality attained by so-called "backward" countries, such as India, Tibet, and Thailand (I mention these as examples because they are unique in the world right now): "We are used to concentrating our attention on the economic backwardness of these countries, on Indian poverty and the legacies of its caste system, on Tibet's illiteracy and the imperfections of its family structure. Meanwhile, we consciously keep our eyes shut to the other side of their cultures; a side which sustains the strength of their cities, centered around temples, which embody tremendous beauty and enlightenment. Through such soaring genius, the face of earth has been beautified by magnificent architecture, thanks to which, holy rivers flow through these countries between banks crowned with countless memorials to human striving towards spirit, light, and beauty. We forget that side of Indian life without which any peoples of the world could not have freed themselves from centuries-long enslavement: the methods of non-violence – the most ethical methods ever implemented."

If the Russian people choose the path of spiritual enrichment; if they resurrect their culture, while keeping close contact to other countries, then material well-being will be reached with even greater ease. Labor will be perceived as a glorious creation. Upon reaching a certain level of development, Russia will discover and implement a new religion, new teachings built on the doctrines of the past and those of modernity, a new view of world order. She will enrich other cultures through her experience. She will deliver a highest truth for which she has been being prepared for over many centuries: the truth of a world Brotherhood, because every state carries within it the evils and dangers of war. The ideal shall manifest itself in concrete reality. Then *all* humanity (it must be a universal action because the Brotherhood, surrounded by state structures will immediately be attacked and conquered by them) will freely and voluntarily enter a new epoch, in the Spring of which Russia had stood.

I wish to end this essay with a poem which reflects my sense of homeland, of Russia:

> "In the high temple, in the heavens,
>   She came, who through the depths of her eyes,
>   And by the strength of thought, in these wild forests,
>   Breathed life into us.
>
> Through love she gave birth,
> To holy men, to heroes,
> She granted them the power of wisdom.
> And waited for them at the open doors.
>
> And all who loved her in return,
> Whose hearts burned with heavenly fire,
> Received in return great power,
> The power of a joy, unconquerable by sword."

Chernevsky, Artyom

GREAT RUSSIA ON THE BRINK

The social order of the state of the ancient Slavs was, for a long period of time, the Obshina system. In its durability and stability, it slowed the class-stratification of Russian society, despite the development of high levels of industrial relations.

Agriculture was the cornerstone of economic life. There was also some cattle raising, forestry, and hunting. Military spoils were another contribution: leaders, and their bands of warriors, undertook raids in Byzantium, where they took slaves and items of luxury. Druzhina (the military guard of the nobility) began to spring from these warring bands and became the foundation of the noble's legitimacy and power.

Such was the ancient *Rus*, until 862 A.D., when three Viking nobles, Rurik, Siteus, and Truvor, were invited to rule Novgorod. Under their leadership a feudal state began to form. This period is particularly interesting because of the appearance of an early legal document – the code of law, *The Russian Truth*. One of its tenets was an unambiguous answer to the question of the worth of a human life in Russia. For the murder of a Ludin (a freeman) one had to pay forty Griven (currency of the period) and for the murder of a Smerd (lower classes), the penalty was eight Griven. This period also witnessed an intense cultural evolution, which was forcefully interrupted by the *Baty Khun's* invasion.

The Russia of that day was riddled by in-fighting, which was characteristic of this period of feudal fragmentation. Russian nobles could not assemble armies large enough to prevent the invasion, because some of the them rejoiced in the misfortune of their neighbors, thinking that the war would not touch them. After numerous losses by fragmented Druzhinas, it became clear that freedom from the Tartar Mongol yoke could only be achieved through unity. Therefore, the threat of the Golden Horde sped up the process of unifying Russia around Moscow. This unification was achieved through differing means. Moscow and Tver had advantages over the other provinces, but found themselves in very similar situations. The balances tipped in Moscow's favor when Ivan Kalita, who was unscrupulous enough to use Mongol troops, put down a popular rebellion in Tver. Moreover, while strengthening and enlarging his holdings, Kalita did not have a larger state-oriented goal, was only guided by his personal quest for power, and was basically a faithful vassal of the Horde. His grandson, Dmitry Donskoy, due to the strong efforts of the Moscow Boyars and Aleksii (the Metropolit of the Russian Orthodox Church), was granted the Yarlyk (the Hun edict) to rule the county of Moscow and was able to establish a treaty with the Suzdal-Nizhny Novgorod ruler. Moscow's prestige was further embellished by the construction of a new whitestone Kremlin. In 1375, the Moscow-Tver war broke out. The major forces of the Russian lands rallied around Moscow. After an unsuccessful defense of Tver, its ruler was forced to recognize Moscow's rule.

Therefore, the Count of Moscow, Dmitry, had no opponents in Russian proper, and his hands were freed for the struggle against the Horde. On September 8, 1380, on the shores of the river Nepryadva, a battle took place, which was later named the Kulikov Battle. It is characteristic that under the flags of Dmitiri, besides the warriors of Vladimir and Moscow counties, there were also warriors from Rostov, Yaroslavl, Murom, Pskov, Bryansk, Polotsk, and Trubchevsk. Only the counts of Suzdal-Nizhny Novgorod, and those of Tver did not send troops, since they were weakened by the previous wars. Despite this, the armies of Dmitry included all the major Russian forces of the time. The victory on Kulikov field did not free the Russian lands from the Horde's yoke, but became a breaking point in the history of the struggle and showed the necessity for the unification of the Russian lands for resistance against outside threats.

Later, the rulers of Russia tried to push the limits of the Russian Empire by joining neighboring lands in need of protection. In the 16th century, the addition of lands east of the Urals began. The bright personality of the period was the Cossack leader Yermak Timofeevich. After the first major defeat of the Hun Kuchum's army by Yermak, many local rulers expressed their desires to join Russia. Through military cunning, Kuchum destroyed Yermak, but the campaigns of the Cossack leader undoubtedly laid the foundation for the eventual inclusion of Siberia in the Russian Empire.

In May 1648, Bogdan Khmelnitsky expressed the desire of the Ukrainian peoples to rejoin Russia. In June 1653 he received documents of agreement; and by March 27, 1654, the acceptance of the Ukraine was complete with a guarantee for the rights and freedom of its population. In 1667 the agreement was further solidified by Russian-Polish agreement. Herein the Smolensk, Chernigov, and Starodub regions were annexed. It was at this juncture that Poland acknowledged the Ukraine/Kiev additions.

Peter the Great also played a major role in the expansion of Russian borders. After the Northern War (1700-21), Russia not only became a seafaring empire, but under the favorable conditions, made a deal to exchange Finland, and 1.5 million rubles, for Leifland, Ainland, Ingermanland, part of Karleya and Vyborg, and the islands of Azel and Dago, which had belonged to Sweden.

We also cannot avoid mentioning the "mother-ruler", Catherine II. During her reign, there were second and third divisions of Poland. After the second, Russia acquired most of the Ukraine and the central part of Belorussia, and, after the third – western Ukraine and Belorussia, Lithuania and Kurlandia. Therefore, despite her reactionary policies, Catherine the Great also added to the development of the Russian Empire.

From 1801-04, Georgia joined Russia, which put an end to the feudal infighting in that country and gave it protection from outside aggression. During the reign of Alexander I, 1804-6, the region of Azerbaidjan was added. After the War of 1812, Russia annexed Moldavia, excepting its western part. During this same period, Finland joined. Nicholas I, in the first half of the 19th century, finished the process of the voluntary addition of Kazakhstan, and began adding other regions of Middle Asia. But as this expansion progressed, the size of the state grew in importance as an issue, because, in addition to its greater size, it manifested an ever-increasing bureaucracy, and, therefore, growing opportunity for corruption and bribery. The rotting feudal regimes had not satisfied the needs of the growing state; and the Czarist government had resisted, to its utmost, any change of the status quo in its attempts to maintain its grip on power. As a result of this decay of the government apparatus came the loss of the Crimean War and the loss of the southern part of Bessarabia (Romania).

A revolutionary situation in Russia began to develop, because the Czarist government was unable to reorganize its apparatus effectively to administrate the country. There was a growing dissatisfaction with the status quo, not only amongst the intelligentsia, but amongst the masses as well. Peter the Great, Catherine the Great, Alexander I, and Nicholas I all immortalized their names in expanding and developing the Russian Empire through the methods available to them in their times. Bur serfdom could not satisfy the growing social demands of the society. With the help of the reforms of 1861, the revolution was only delayed. If the Czarists could have overcome the revolution later on, it would have still been an inevitable occurrence.

And so... Revolution! What kind of social order would replace monarchy. A large number of parties participated in the political struggle: Reactionaries, Anarchists, Social Democrats, Social Revolutionaries, Constitutional Democrats, Bolsheviks... We all know the outcome of the struggle – the absolute victory of the Bolsheviks and the annihilation of all other parties. The following years were the years of the "prosperous USSR", and are well-described in the political propaganda of its time. The only fact which the literature of that time fails to explain is the decay of the Russian economic system and the departure of the USSR from an international position of leadership. In an analysis of this situation, let us use the same methods used by Soviet historians in their analysis of the decaying Czarist monarchy.

The dissolution of the USSR was not caused by a single, clearly-defined reason. Even today, the lists of causes is far from complete.

In general, "the theory of building socialism in an isolated, single country" had been fully and thoroughly criticized: beginning with the statement "if one decides to build socialism in an isolated country, choose one which you do not pity", and continuing through the fundamental works of L. Trotsky. In his article "On Socialism in a Single Country", he gives a detailed proof of the following logical construction: The basis of socialism is industrialization, since the proletariat is its foundation, and therefore a growing number of economic ties with neighbors emerges. These ties can only be realized through the world market, with its crises, fluctuating prices, and recessions. The planned economy, which is the cornerstone of socialism, could never exist while being tied to such mutating markets. Therefore, in choosing the path of building socialism, a country is unable to attain a desired result and is forced to veer from its original goal.

Of course, there were a few ways to exit the situation, and it is incorrect to blame our political leaders for choosing a wrong path. In the given situation, these leaders could not have made a different choice. This brings us to another problem – could we have had different leaders?

First, I hope that we can remember the difference between poets and politicians. The former are scorned in their lifetimes and praised after they die, while the opposite is true for the latter. Let us try to imagine what kind of people made it into the ruling elite in the USSR. A paradox exists in the fact that, the higher the position a person was in, the further away his thoughts and lifestyle were removed from what the media sought to instill in every citizen of the USSR. Why was there such a discrepancy? In my opinion, it was due to the fact that, after 1917, the number of entrepreneurial individuals had not declined, rather they were forced to find new applications for their talents. The most effective "way to the top" was a rise on the party bureaucratic ladder. Upon admittance to the party, the competitive spirit immediately arose, which was so lacking in our industrial sectors. There was concern with how to avoid the next purge and insure that afterwards there would be an empty chair higher up. As a result, all the pure idealists were left out, and only those came out on top for whom ruling the country was a way to satisfy their own private needs. An example which is characteristic of this, is the struggle between Trotsky and Stalin after the death of Lenin. In the beginning, the "humble one", ready to remain at the end of the list in which Trotsky and Lenin were mentioned first, Stalin, played the Trotskyites against one another, while moving his loyal followers into important administrative positions, and had managed, by small, slow steps to outmaneuver Trotsky, to anathematize him by accusing him of organizing an assassination attempt on M. Gorky! One more reason for the fall of socialism was the fact that the party system started to inhibit the demands of those who made it to the upper echelons. They had to keep themselves within certain limits, because their competitors, relying on the support of the general party membership, would accuse them of bourgeois tendencies and other "deadly sins".

We cannot forget the fact that many capitalist countries were very interested in the destruction of the competitive socialist camp.

And so we have a country attempting achieve the impossible, the rulers of which are mainly interested in their private welfare, while its neighbors passionately desire its demise, and are ready to support any actions towards that goal. The conclusion is a change in the political order. As a consequence the fact that many peoples with different traditions, cultures, and ways of life, having been previously helped in the beginning by military might, and later consolidated by ideology, now have almost nothing to gain by staying with the union. Add a little bit more Western agitation and there would be, instead of a colossus on legs of clay, a pile of shards.

The change in the political order of Russia has one very specific attitude: "First we will destroy the old, and then... " In the present, a very interesting moment is coming. To destroy anything further is dangerous, because the dissatisfaction of the masses could pass the limit, and the situation become uncontrollable. The western political leaders should probably wish that the situation in Russia "freeze" in its present state. Russia is a sellers market, a labor market, a market of natural resources, and a market of intellectual potential. The only thing missing is a small civil war in order to have a reason to either send in "peacekeeping forces", or to gain the ability to grab the power through mediation, under the principle of divide and conquer. A large-scale war, however, considering our nuclear arsenal, is not desired by the world community.

People of Russia, of course, wish for the restoration of the country, but there are no realistic means towards this end, and nobody is taking the people's opinions into account, using it instead as a weapon for political struggle. For example, let us return to the issue of the price of human life in Russia. The situation right now is much more complicated than it was in the ancient Russian state. During times of repression people "disappeared" by the thousands, without a single reaction from society, while, in the present, the death of every soldier in Chechnya, is painted in most tragic colors. It is not because the media exchanged their political dependency for an economic one, but it is because public opinion is led in the direction which is needed by those holding the power (these are not necessarily the government), and the media is the Archimedian lever.

Based on the statements above, let us look at the options for further development of the country. Let us limit ourselves to the possibilities in which the economy develops, because in other cases there will result a reign of chaos which is unlikely to lead to anything good. The development of the economy in a given situation is possible only on the account of foreign investors, or on the account of a powerful spiritual upsurge among the people (this upsurge took place in the 1920's, the 1960's, and was the cause of the breakthroughs in the wars of 1812 and W.W.II). Foreign investors are not interested in the development of a competitive country, therefore we should not count on their help. The fall of the socialist order was followed by the destruction of ideals and a complete loss of faith. During the socialist era, the upsurge of a national effort was also used too often to "catch and leave behind" other countries. Therefore that resource has been completely used up for a generation or two. Also, the present media has too few "rallying points". Even patriotism has left the consciousness of the masses of the population, as have the socialist ideals. Without a spiritual upsurge of the people, rebuilding the economy, under "temporary difficulties"[1], is unrealistic in the present situation, because the majority of people would find themselves below the poverty level, and all the assets would be concentrated in the hands of a small group of those who used to be the leaders in the "stagnation period". Naturally, this would lead to the resurgence of the idea of social "equality", a generally familiar situation in Russian history.

There remains only a single option: the slow improvement of the economy on the accounts of natural resources and the maximum reduction in all state expenditures (space programs, the military, and all state structures). There must be an introduction of a new tax policy, relying mostly on taxes on large property and asset holdings, and an organization of effective ways to control taxation. But all of this is unrealistic under the present government, which fully depends on the owners of large property and capital.

Therefore, we will most likely become a half-colony from which there will be a cheap import of all natural resources, which will be maintained for the purposes of international secu-

---

[1] "Temporary difficulties" was the Communist explanation used to justify hardship during their rule. An anecdote of the Soviet era asked, "What is the most permanent feature of Soviet society?" The answer being "Temporary difficulties."

rity at a level just above poverty. In general, the conclusions have a rather pessimistic character, but, in my opinion, this would be a logical chain of events, in which chance will make its own corrections.

Bibliography

1 Antonov, F.D. Russian Historical Reader, 2nd Edition, Moscow, *Prosveschenie*,1984.

2 Trotsky's Archives, *Terra* 1990.

3 Heroes and Antiheroes of the Fatherland, Edit. V.M. Zabrodin, Moscow, *Inform Express, Russian Gazette, Practica*, 1992.

4 Pavlenko, N.E., Russian Reader, Moscow, *Prosveschenie*, 1989.

5 Sirotkin, V.G., Milestones of Native History, Moscow, *International Relations*, 1991.

6 The Pages of the History of Soviet Society, Edit. A.T. Kinkulkin, Moscow, *Polit Izdat*, 1989.

Chegin, Dmitry

THE ROLE OF THE INTELLIGENTSIA IN THE BREAKDOWN OF RUSSIA

> "Revolutions are not conducted in white gloves." (famous Bolshevik slogan) "Why should we be indignant that counter-revolutions are conducted in hedgehog-needled mittens?"
>
> "Cursed Days", I. Bunin

Russia... Great country, Great Russian people, Great Russian culture. But all of this lies in the past, and will probably never be resurrected. To whom do we owe this favor? The Zionist conspiracy? The long arm of the CIA? Or the collective hatred of "developed" countries towards us? I think not. We owe all of this to the so-called "blossom of Russian thought and culture" – the intelligentsia.

Russia gave the world many great writers: Pushkin and Tolstoy, Dostoevsky and Turgenev, Griboedov and Bunin. And what a multitude of great scientists, musicians and artists: Mendeleev, Popov, Mussorgsky, Glinka, Tchaikovsky, Repin, Serov, Shishkin. Thanks to these individuals, Russian people attained high stature in world culture. However, the Great culture also created a group of people who, by their very existence, discredit culture.

228

"We had all studied a little bit, something and somehow" wrote Pushkin, and this, in my opinion, is the most exact definition of the intelligentsia. They started to speak of culture and art, and then, of politics. Attaining only a superficial knowledge of these subjects, they have begun to reason. By doing so, they paved the way for their own destruction.

I will separate the intelligentsia into two parts: pre-revolutionary, and "sovok" (pejorative slang for Soviet). These two groups are united by only one feature – a deep dislike of the existing order. I will study this feature of the intelligentsia, beginning with the former.

The Russian empire manifested a powerful multinational state. Multiple reformers slowly but steadily moved the nation towards a constitutional monarchy. There was rapid growth in industry and agriculture. Russian nobility produced many great leaders in culture and art, economics and politics. Despite its wavering, the Romanov dynasty was leading the country towards its "bright future". However, there existed a whole subclass of people who hated this social order – the intelligentsia. I think that characterization of this group would be best served by the words of I. Bunin: "Long ago a worldwide bureau for the creation of human happiness was established... you need spies, traitors, the corrupters of enemy armies? Here – we have already shown our abilities in the described venues. Do we need to "provoke" something? Sure thing – more experience in lowlife provocation, you'll not find anywhere else... "

You might ask": "Are not these words too strong?" I disagree, because Bunin saw the results of intelligentsia action.

I think that Bunin's words describe these actions well: "There was a narod (a people), 160 million strong, who ruled a sixth of the world, and what a portion – containing untold riches, and progressing with incredible speed! And these people were told over and over again, for one hundred years, that their only salvation was to take land from thousands of landowners, land holdings which were rapidly diminishing." Is it not true that this description can be well-applied to the present?

And here are the intelligentsia's representatives, her leaders: alcoholic Balmont; pitiful, half-crazy Blok; and Bryusov with his egomania. At the turn of the twentieth century, while Tolstoy, Leskov, and Chekhov were still alive, they declared that art was in decline. Initially calling themselves "modernists", those idols of the intelligentsia soon divided into smaller groups: symbolists, acmeists, futurists, imaginists. And if the majority of the first members of these groups were intelligentsia by birth, later there was an appearance of many Mayakovsky-types.

Indeed it was the intelligentsia which was spawning the revolutionaries – "whole generations of boys and girls played with secret linotypes... and continuously fanned the flames of hatred of the landowners, and of common men... ." In 1914, at the beginning of the First World War, members of the intelligentsia proclaimed: "I am afraid of a Russian victory. I am afraid that wild Russia, with its hundred million strong belly, will fall on Europe." Chekhov said of them: "They are big, strong men, they should be put in disciplinary units."

And it finally happened. In February 1917, the so long-awaited revolution came to pass... The czar was overthrown, the nobility was destroyed. The intelligentsia came into power.

First, the constitutional democrats, later the socialists. These people understood perfectly that they had been brought into power by the riff-raff of the Petersburg garrison, and immediately catered to them. The breakdown of discipline in the army, the loss of control over the country, and lawlessness became the results of the "fruitful" rule of the intelligentsia.

Narod was negative towards the revolution, but was gradually corrupted by the propagandists and by the atmosphere of permissiveness. Even though the revolutionaries sometimes said things of this nature: "I come on to you insolently... 'Tovaricsh, Tovaricsh!... but, really, I should be reprimanded for that!' If anyone should be elected,... it should be you, Comrade Bunin."

And then God's punishment came – Bolshevik rule began. What ensued was such that the period of provisional government seemed a paradise, to many, in comparison. Executions, murders, Cheka ("the extraordinary commission", i.e. the secret police), robberies... People came to power who were very distant, far-removed from the intelligentsia. The dream of the proletariat came true: "To break the head of the fabrikant (plant owner), turn out his pockets, and become a worse bastard than the fabrikant himself." However, they not only broke the heads of the fabrikants, the landowners, and officers, but also those of the intelligentsia.

And that was the end of the pre-revolutionary intelligentsia as an entity. Some, like, Gippius and Merezhkovsky, had noticed that individuality was beginning to disappear. Their relationship to the revolution could be described by Gippius' following pronouncement: "Revolution is a slavery, a physical impoverishment of the soul, of thought, and of individuality, that is, of all that distinguishes a human from a beast... " These people believed that they could destroy Bolshevism, and thousands of them found their deaths in the flanks of the white armies. After the Red Victory, they emigrated and quietly died out dreaming of the return of the monarchy in Russia.

Others, such as Blok, Balmont, and Gumilev had welcomed "October", but soon understood that, against the background of murders, robberies, and pogroms, their exclamations of "Listen to the music of revolution!" was at the very least ridiculous, if not horrible. Their ends were tragic: Blok went insane, Gumilev was executed for counter-revolutionary conspiracy, and Balmont emigrated.

Others, like Pasternak, Bulgakov, Esenin, Akhmatova, and Tsvetaeva (who had emigrated and returned in 1940) stayed in the USSR and became the best representatives of its literature. Their destinies were tragic as well, and I will describe them a little later.

But there was a group of the intelligentsia which followed Mayakovsky and Gorky. Bigger opportunists the world had never seen. Even though they consistently painted all that was "old" in black, they still did not escape the scythe of Communist terror. However, the period of sovdepia (order of Soviet Deputies, ed.) was coming to an end, and absolute Bolshevism (similar to absolute monarchism) was looming on the horizon. With the end of the civil war the intelligentsia as a social class was destroyed or at least greatly diminished. Despite the accelerated work of higher educational institutions in the 1920s-30s, and the large number of graduates, the intelligentsia was not beng reborn. The graduates of the Worker's Department (RABFAK) and the universities of the USSR did not attempt to associate themselves with the past: "We will build our new world." (Internationale, international Communist hymn)

The intelligentsia was quietly dying out and decaying, loosing its leaders: Esenin was murdered and Mayakovsky died (poets, ed.). But the evil 30s were coming, together with the prisons of the NKVD. "Absolute Bolshevism" was roaring...

As early as the 20s in the USSR, they started to get rid of the intelligentsia. In 1922, S.N. Bulgakov, N.A. Berdayev, I.A. Ilyin, and many others (300) were exiled. At the end of the 20s a consistent destruction of this sub-class had started: Palchinsky, Khrenikov, Fedotov, Gvozdyov, and many others died tragically.

The 20s saw the start of terror against the intelligentsia: all of her representatives in the Central Committee of the Communist Party were murdered, her leaders and inspirers were executed or exiled, M.A. Bulgakov, author of "Master Margarita" died, M. Tsvetaeva committed suicide, and O. Mandelshtam died in jail. This completely destroyed the remains of the pre-revolutionary intelligentsia.

This part of the intelligentsia disappeared immediately after the loss of its environment. Who was supporting her before the revolution, who gave her the right to exist? City folk, nobility, peasants, office workers! With their disappearance, the ground under the feet of the intelligentsia disappeared as well. "New" Soviet men did not have any use for intelligentsia. The flower of Soviet literature and art: ... N.A. Ostrovsky, V. Kaverin, D. Furmanov, and A. Fadeyev were completely unconcerned with the fate of the intelligentsia. No wonder the simple folk forgot them. Millions of citizens of the USSR, ready for sacrifice, having faith in "the idea" could not, and did not want to support the shards of pre-revolutionary life. Despite the repressions, Soviet citizens were merging into unity, the empire of the USSR grew and strengthened, "absolute Bolshevism" grew in power.

With the beginning of the Great Patriotic War, Soviet people unified. Despite initial losses, millions of prisoners of war, and the larger territorial losses, they continued the struggle. Loosing its best people to the hardships of war, Russia nevertheless triumphed over German fascism. The patriotism of the war welded the people of the Soviet Union together to serve the Communist Party.

However, the victory also had negative consequences: the army and the people saw life in the west. The high standard of living was in sharp contrast to ration cards and communal housing. The people came into contact with western intelligentsia and Russian émigrés. The contagion of free thinking had penetrated the souls of the people.

"Absolute Bolshevism" had always dealt decisively and cruelly with dissent. In Leningrad, the new center of the intelligentsia, mass arrests were made and many people joined the ranks of the Gulag populations. There was an extensive smear campaign in the press against Pasternak and Akhmatova. The contagion was stomped out.

However, as time passed, the enthusiasm of people diminished. They worked and received nothing in return for their labor. Despite the secret police, a distrust of the Communist "idea" began to develop among the people. With the death of

234

Stalin, absolute Bolshevism ceased to exist, and the following Soviet leaders preserved the essence of its order, without using its methods. There came a time of deficits and corruption, prevailing bribes and nepotism. Seeing the luxury of the bureaucrats, the population increasingly lost faith in Communism. The era of super achievements, socialist competition, free labor, had left with no return. Laziness began a victorious march through the USSR. There probably was not a single kitchen where the Soviet order, and its characteristics was not criticized.

It was at this point that the second part of the intelligentsia – sovok – came into being. However, in sharp contrast to pre-revolutionary education, Soviet colleges provided only foundations for specialized knowledge. This is how many people appeared, who graduated from polytechnic institutes and called themselves intelligentsia. But their souls were "deeply sympathetic" to the people as their predecessors. The contagion of the intelligentsia quickly spread across the country.

In the 70s and 80s the USSR reached the acme of its development. A gigantic army, nuclear weapons, the KGB, and propaganda safeguarded Communist order. Western countries were even afraid to openly criticize goings-on in the USSR. All, it seemed, was going well.

But there were also signs of decay. In the struggle against dissidents and the intelligentsia, the authorities had used verdicts based on laughable pretenses: slandering of the Soviet way of life, and parasitism (a first offense drew six months of incarceration). This showed weakness in the existing order. Even small public demonstrations by inakomyslyacshiy ("those who

235

think differently") appeared. Even underground monarchists appeared in the USSR!

Russian science and culture produced two idols of the intelligentsia: Sakharov and Solzhenitsin. These two individuals attained glory through their struggle against Communism and were repressed.

Solzhenitsin became the leader of one group of the intelligentsia. The aims of their position could be defined as "democratic statehood", federalism, for a strong and powerful Russia.

Sakharov became the inspirer of a different group, who maintained that Russians were inherently totalitarian people and needed to be changed. However, they also gave recognition to the greatness of our culture.

A third group consisted of people of the Voinovich-type. Her followers wanted to transform Russian society along American lines. For that goal, they were ready to abandon the past. This group hoped, more than anything, for help from the USA and the West.

I. Brodsky (Russian Nobel Prize poet) was also a secret ideologist. His group preached democratization and the freedom of self-expression.

A fifth group consisted of people such as E. Gaidar and his contemporary allies. These people sought to "fix" Russia by transforming the economy. For the sake of this idea, they were willing to sacrifice politics.

Yet another group consisted of a collection of different nationalists, except, of course, Russians. Their actions consisted of "raising the self-consciousness of their peoples". The meticulously poured invective on Russians and all that is Russian.

Kovalev and Novodvorskaya inspired a final group of intelligentsia. Their main task was the struggle with "totalitarianism", and all expressions of Russian self-consciousness. This group sold its Homeland wholesale and retail, and betrayed and slandered it at every turn. With the Soviet invasion of Afghanistan, the influence of the intelligentsia grew drastically. The books and newspapers of "Samizdat" circulated among the population. Ideologists of the intelligentsia and Western secret task forces were cleverly undermining the USSR, using all methods – from the bible to jokes – towards that end. Members of the intelligentsia had even penetrated the state apparatus and the inner circle of the members of the politburo.

When Gorbachev came into power, the intelligentsia gained power as well by discrediting the party nomenclature's anti-alcohol decree. Having powerfully developed, they began to break down Communist order. Such people as Shevardnadze and Yakovlev became the conductors of the intelligentsia's ideas at the helm of power.

Concurrently, Boris Yeltsin emerged. He was the conductor of the ideas of the young, reformer-nomenclature. These people wanted to take power from the party bureaucracy, but were "beaten into ashes" by it.

But, the party bureaucracy had also pushed away the intelligentsia from power. The result of the rule by the "old guard" became operations in the fight against nationalism: Baku, Tblisi, Fergana, Karabakh, Vilnius. They attempted to find support amongst Russians by playing on their feelings of nationalism, and also implemented a currency reform, as well as a sharp price increase. As a result of their policies, the Communists lost support among the people.

The events of 19-21 August finally undermined Communist authority. The army refused to disperse the people and the whole order collapsed. The Party lost its power and the empire collapsed as well, an empire which had been sustained for 70 years by "iron and blood". This was the end of the epoch of Soviet order. Its entire value system was destroyed and the giant empire broken down – and all of this is to the credit of the intelligentsia.

However, her victory was not full. Despite the joyful shouting and euphoria of the first days of democracy, why is it that the following words are still pertinent today:

" 'An old, totally decayed regime has fallen with no return... ' – but why then are all horrified by the reaction and restoration?" This is Bunin again, even though he was speaking of the monarchy.

Democrats and their leader, E. Gaidar, started bringing the tenets of the intelligentsia to life: appeasement in foreign and internal reform. Attempts to develop efficient venues for the economy directly clashed with a central characteristic of Russian nature: laziness. Appeasement in foreign policy brought about the destruction of the army and the defense industry, and attempts to balance the budget placed unjustified demands upon the economic committees. This lead to the departure of the intelligentsia from the echelons of power, due to pressure from the supreme Soviet, and its replacement by the nomenclature.

Her representatives began conducting more nationalistic politics despite widespread criticism. However, with the nomenclature in power, bribery and nepotism among bureaucrats flourished. The majority of the intelligentsia continued to support Yeltsin.

The events of October 1993 brought a sharp division in the ranks of the intelligentsia. One part, with Gaidar as its leader, continued to support Yeltsin, while the other, behind Yavlinsky, condemned the former for the violation of human rights.[1] The schism between the intelligentsia and the nomenclature was used by the Communists and the Nationalists, and their positions had been strengthening since August 1991. The intelligentsia had destroyed all former ideals, but could not bring new ones into people's consciousness, and... it began... :

"In the spiritual darkness of the young, unbalanced and dissatisfied people, seditious political swings easily appeared. ... And now they reemerge again, in gigantic magnitude... the spirit of materialism, uncontrolled will, and raw self-interest have descended destructively into Russia."

The war in Chechnya, which was begun in the name of the re-establishment of Russian unity, completely undermined the intelligentsia. Russian intelligentsia then parted with Yeltsin and took as their motto Novodvorskaya ("We need no great empire, rather a small democratic Russia.")

---

[1] Specifically, the dissolution and violent takeover of Parlament by troops loyal to Yeltsin

However, they fail to understand that narod does not support them. Despite the massive hysterics of the press and television the population and the army are overcoming the syndrome of Russian "inferiority". Russian self-consciousness is on the rise and this is well-understood by the presidents of fake "republics". The era of a great, imperial unitarian State is drawing near.

The cause of the intelligentsia's failure as a social sub-class lies in the absence of a consistent philosophic world outlook (mirovozrenie). Throughout its existence, the intelligentsia claimed that the West was superior. But they overlooked the fact that the Russian mentality will never allow such a level of degradation and destruction of morality in its society. Russians always feel the need for a strong power and good leadership. The dreams of revolution as the means of reforming life toward a better, democratic ideal were canceled by the events of 1917 and 1991. The people would only accept revolution as the means towards establishing a strong authority.

The intelligentsia did play somewhat of a positive role as well. Over a long period of time it consistently brought education to the masses. The state must use these beginnings for its own purposes. The best the intelligentsia can do now is to leave politics and cease its activities. Her best representatives must help the state to overcome the sedition and turmoil which currently reigns. Only with her help will we be able to build a new great and undivided empire, one which I hope will be more humane.

Shmakov, Dmitry

RECURRENT TURMOIL

That's the way it is, in this land of mine...
All is not to the glory of God, all is not like everywhere else...
On this land of mine there is the sickle instead of grain,
Smoke instead of sun, the yoke instead of freedom

K.Kinchev

June 12,1990. On this date the "Declaration of the State Sovereignty of Russia" was ratified. Since then June 12 has become a holiday – Independence Day. And it is from that date that new political years are being counted in the new Russia. More than four years have passed and we are still not clear on our political attitude towards this historical fact. Of course, due to the accelerated attempts and not-always-justified actions which have shaken the very foundation of the state power and social order, the country has suffered many substantial losses. The fact remains that Russia never had the time for gradual reform: the abscess matures for a long time, and painfully ("It takes a long time to harness the horses"), until finally the flesh is torn for the necessary operation. History did not even afford Peter the Great the least opportunity to implement temperate change in the face of the intense pressures of the issues of the survival of the Russian people and their independent course of development. And so it goes on forever.

We will take this risk of stating that the history of Russia has three cycles, which would be as follow:

1. Sedition
2. The Ditch
3. Stagnation

There is sedition in Russia now and Russia longs for 'the ideal'. We are going through hard times which will continue, it seems, for some time. It has happened many times before and just as many times, Russia overcame its misfortunes, becoming a great country once again. After the glorious sunrise come neglect and inertia. At the end of the cycle there is decline of social order and the necessity of reform begins to grow. The circle closes and social evolution starts anew. This point of view is probably not new and the formula stated need not apply exclusively to Russia (which it seems is able to satisfy any social/political theory with its abundance of historical tendencies and precedents); I am simply expressing my opinion.

Russia has many hypotheses. In principle, the theme of this essay, embodied in its title "Russia: Yesterday, Today Tomorrow", does not limit the choice of specific subject matter. This is why, when speaking of Russia, I will take into consideration its three main components – ideas, people, and power.

Nothing is to be proved here, we seek only to express certain thoughts.

Russia is dominated right now by economic, political, and most of all, spiritual crises. The Russian soul is in a state of chaos, veiled in clouds of smoke. Its mystery remains impenetrable even to Russians. We will not attempt to analyze and judge this soul here. A great expert on the Russian soul, F.M. Dostoevsky, in his own time, stated "To study, to understand, and to describe the human soul is impossible, nobody can do it." Only poets and artists take the correct approach (though even they will not get the desired results) through revelation and creativity. No positive, well-known science, in principle, can penetrate the sphere and spiritual life of a human; positivism and rational objectivity is powerless before any of our inner worlds. Therefore we will consciously avoid any analysis of this kind. In spiritual space it is much easier to operate with ideas and theories which govern the rational part of social consciousness. This is why it is said that human history is the history of ideas.

In the Russian's soul there is a struggle between two super-ideas which determine the meaning and content of all other ideas: Perun (pre-Christian Russian god) and God. If for some time the cult of the wild forces of nature predominate, man worships the Beast; when the higher forces triumph, man worships the creator. Paganism and Christianity go hand in hand in Russian life, mixing and intertwining, and simultaneously resisting each other ("... they are merging and combining, fatefully mixing and fatefully struggling"). These two antagonistic entities of Russian spiritual life do not possess well-defined borders in time. Obviously paganism had not ended when the population of Kiev tasted God's first blessing of baptism under the watchful eye of the prince's militia. We know how hard it was for ancient Russia to incorporate Christianity. Annals testify of the bloody rebellion against the "Greek Faith" under the banners of great Slavic pagan spirit. Behind that spirit stood the centuries-long tradition of ancestral Slavic peoples (living in the forests and steppes from the Carpathians to the Urals), as well as the ancient Slavs. The strength of the Slavic soul is paganism. The rites and rituals, fairytales and myths, heroes and gods, their way of life and freedom-loving character were all paganistic, since their historical roots lay in the forests, fields, steppes, and lakes. As does every young ethnos, the Slavs had their own paganistic system. But, at a certain stage of development, there is a need for a revolution in spiritual life. Idolatry must be replaced by the cult of the symbol of a singular, higher power. Then there will be the development of an economy, state institutions, and art; from which will evolve an integration into world trade, economy, and culture, the exchange of ideas and knowledge, and entrance into the world community. This, of course, is not a result of the acceptance of world religion; even though it is required, it is not a sufficient condition. In general, the cosmopolitanism of a religion is an indicator of the civilization of its people. The continual renunciation of monotheistic world religion, in favor of paganistic cults, leads to the stagnation of all internal processes, to the decline and disappearance of that ethnos.

The true depth of the Russian soul is full of paganistic essence. One should not think that we are special, since other nations, like the Germans, Franks, and Anglo-Saxons had their own forest gods, elves, fairies, sorcerers, and trolls before accepting "Roman Faith" in due time. German national identity is built on the cult of heroes and being chosen by God, which is the eclecticism of paganism and cosmopolitanism. The Russian

244

ideology which emerged, and still serves to fulfill internal and external sociopolitical goals, consists of the same distorted mixture of the two super-ideas. The notion of the "Third Rome" conquered the Muscovite tzardom only after the inheritance of the Byzantine title, through the line of Sofia Palaeologa[1]. The ideologists of the Muscovite state, the first of which was Ivan the Terrible, eloquently and precisely (as ideologists of a totalitarian regime) substantiated the Russian rights on the world stage of "The New Rome". The constant inner impulse of the existence of a nation found itself in the Russian idea of messianism and "the chosen people", even though the idea of the "Third Rome" does not seriously concern anyone in Russia now.

The struggle between westernizers and Slavophiles was nothing else but a confrontation between two ideals, western cosmopolitanism and Russian messianism.

There is a lack of ideas today (really it is a lack of brains). Of course, in troubled times there are troubled ideas which call for the worship of the golden calf, the cult of success and respectability. Russians no longer want to be "the great ones", they have been overrun by mercantilism. Some still dream of resurrecting the "Great Russia", but a great country is based on a great people, great in the simplicity of their souls, in the heroics of their spiritual trials, and in their everyday labor. The idea of creating a democratic civil society and a constitutional state, together with economic progress, has yet to capture the hearts of Russians. We Russians, who are subconsciously proud to be the most ungoverned and politically free people, have a hard time accepting that the facts of history do not give reason to ac-

---

[1] Niece of the last Byzantine Emperor and a wife of Ivan III

245

cept democratic traditions in Russian social life. However,
not for the unremitting attacks by hoards of enemies, the ea
Slavic state would be the most democratic in the world, eve
now. (Let us remember that it was the Slavs who invente
Veche, the popular assembly, as well as the trial by jury
During the wars, community rule ceased to exist and the exec
tive power was consolidated in the hands of a single ruler. Aft
wartime he did not want to give up this unlimited power. Th
Veche undoubtedly fought against this, but could not always se
its way to victory, since new enemies prevented a resolution
this internal struggle. In this way, the "chosen prince" gradual
was entrusted with the powers of a monarch. Later the Tzars
Moscow and the emperors of St. Petersburg would not be bu
dened with feelings of duty and responsibility towards the pe
ple.

There is another aspect specific to the Russian way
Obshinnost (communality). As the historian Aksakov say
"Obshinnost is the necessity to live together in consent and lov
understood by every member of Obshinna, of community, as th
higher law, obligatory for all, and finding its justification in i
self and not in personal desires of the individual. This is the li
of Obshinna in its essence: it is not based on individuality an
could not be based on it, but it assumes a highest act of freedo
and consciousness – self abnegation."

Previously Russia was saved from political and spiritual il
ness by the instinct of national self -consciousness. This ha
been destroyed over the last century and is the reason Russia
being tossed like a wood splinter in the murky ocean of politic
passions, and it is unclear on which shore it will lan

246

Unfortunately we have no ideology now. And to live without ideology is to live without ideals. "Idealism is the staff which raises men from the four-legged position."

Russia's rulers have always been negligent in expending the forces of her people, and the present ones, it seems, have no clue as to the reasons behind the present sacrifices. Chechnya is the drama which has put into question all that we have gained over the last three years of hardship. It could turn out that we have acquired only a certain acceptance of the features of democracy (parliament, free elections, free media), but not its institutions. Some experts espouse the opinion that the present Russian ruling elite has already proved its inability to create a stable state and conditions for normal social development.

Pessimism, as is well-known, is a social evil; people are moved by hopes. The destiny of Russia is a transformation, not from one happiness to another, but from one hope to the next. Truly,"Russia cannot be comprehended by the mind." And so, as is always the case in troubled times, we only have the hope that now, unseen but powerfully, something new is being born, something great.

I once heard the following story. During the meeting between Napoleon and Alexander I, in Erfurt, the Russian emperor asked Speransky, the author of the first project of the Russian constitution, how he liked being "beyond the boarders" (of Russia). He replied: "We have better people, but here there are superior institutions."

We do indeed have better people. Samuel Beckett, in one of his plays about people crushed by materialism, has the following scene. A man is sitting, vacantly observing his hands... They are used to doing everything by "hand" there, without inspiration. Here, we might be idle, but we are inspired. Indeed we are not interested in hands. That is not how we create. The essence of Russia is soul. The body is rudimentary growth. It is worse now, we have started to be burdened by the "body"...

There has always been theft in Russia. Now there is more. This means they are stealing even their own future. In this transformational, crisis-laden moment, the majority of people who have strong common sense must remain silent, since the smart and reasonable man cannot do anything until he sorts out all the details; until he is fully assured of all his thoughts, words, and actions. Serious people are benumbed now, but this is all just accumulating strength. Meanwhile, while the "deep waters" are quiet, on the surface the obscene dark foam is boiling.

The more effective the laws concerned with protecting the weak and holding the powerful in check are, the more civilized the given state. From the point of view of social human rights norms, Russia is populated with barbarians. These Russian barbarians have two curses: "... below is the power of darkness, above is the darkness of power." "A strong hand at the wheel of government is the national tradition; together with submissiveness and obedience, imposed on the freedom-loving Russian people through whip and sword over the ages. Should we be surprised, then, by the extreme degree of irresponsibility and mass dependence on social programs, which have become characteristic of this nation. "Nobody does anything, and does not intend to."

So what is yesterday, today, and tomorrow in Russia? We know a lot about the present situation in Russia. Thank God we are not blind. But was there a "yesterday" and will there be a "tomorrow"; and if so, what are they?

We have chance to judge the past, but we do not have the right, even though we often forget this fact. (There are many examples testifying to this) At the same time we should not compulsively hold on to the roots, without paying attention to anything else, and without gaining anything new. One should not build national galleries out of national achievements; it is important that they belong to the people. Not to acquire is to lose. And that leads to entropy, the struggle against which is the foremost task of humankind.

However, it is fruitless and meaningless to build illusions about the future, since it does not exist in reality, as does not the past – only the present exists, and man wants to change it, to build a heaven on earth. But utopias spring up from inability to sort out the present...

There is a recurrent sedition in Russia now... The prediction of the future seems to be an ungrateful undertaking. "Collapse" has happened. There is nothing new in sight which is able to move us from this standstill. It is not clear which idea will conquer our minds and hearts and determine our future path...

"Russia, where are you racing to? Answer me! There is no answer. The bells are tinkling and filling the air with their wonderful pealing; the air is torn and thundering as it turns to wind; everything on earth comes flying past and, looking askance at her, other peoples and states move aside and make way."
Nikolai Gogol

Katya Goryunova and her son Ivan, Nizhny, 1992. It was Katya who made the project possible in Russia.

Survey results

The survey conducted among the participants of the essay contest (43), consisted of answering 11 multiple-choice questions and one write-in question.

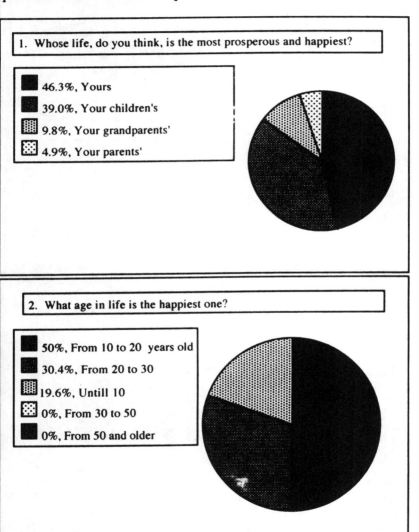

1. Whose life, do you think, is the most prosperous and happiest?

■ 46.3%, Yours
■ 39.0%, Your children's
▦ 9.8%, Your grandparents'
▩ 4.9%, Your parents'

2. What age in life is the happiest one?

■ 50%, From 10 to 20 years old
■ 30.4%, From 20 to 30
▦ 19.6%, Untill 10
▩ 0%, From 30 to 50
■ 0%, From 50 and older

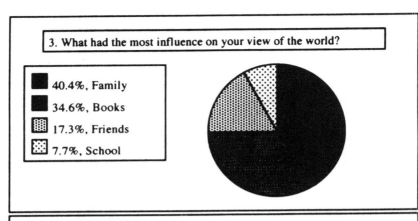

3. What had the most influence on your view of the world?

- 40.4%, Family
- 34.6%, Books
- 17.3%, Friends
- 7.7%, School

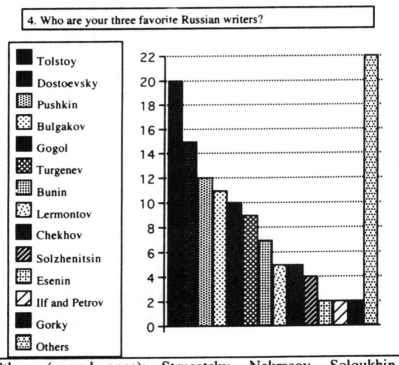

4. Who are your three favorite Russian writers?

- Tolstoy
- Dostoevsky
- Pushkin
- Bulgakov
- Gogol
- Turgenev
- Bunin
- Lermontov
- Chekhov
- Solzhenitsin
- Esenin
- Ilf and Petrov
- Gorky
- Others

Others (named once): Strugatsky, Nekrasov, Soloukhin, Asadov, Sholokhov, Chernyshevsky, Tyutchev, Suvorov, Klyuchevskyi, Bryusov, Pavlov, Solovyov, Daniil Andreev, Leonov, Ostrovsky, Akhmatova, Zamyatin, Griboedov, Ilyin, Kuprin, Kaverin, Brodsky

5. Who is your favorite of the following political leaders?

- 50%, Peter the Great
- 32.7%, Stolypin
- 5.9%, Aleksander II
- 3.8%, Yeltsin
- 1,9%, Stalin
- 1.9%, Khrushev
- 1.9%, Lenin
- 1.9%, Gorbachev
- 0%, Brezhnev

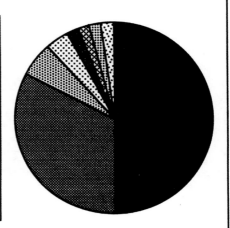

6. What interests you the most?

- 67.4%, Interesting life
- 16.3%, Helping society
- 14.3%, Independence
- 2%, Money

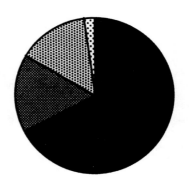

7. What do you think about the break-up of the USSR?

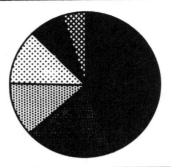

- 43.9%, Bad (must reinstate through democratic process)
- 19.5%, Not bad (for Russia - enough feeding parasites)
- 12.2%, Good (empire collapsed)
- 12.2%, Good (peoples became free)
- 7.3%, Not bad (for the peoples who became independent)
- 4.9%, Bad (must reunite by force, if neccessary)

8. What can improve the state of affairs in Russia?

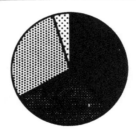

- 38.1%, Strong central power, able to stop crime and mafia
- 28.6%, Further democratization
- 28.6%, Everybody minding his own business and not thinking of politics
- 4.8%, Decentralization of authority

254

9. What is homeland for you?

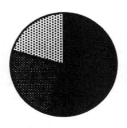

- 54.5%, Russian people
- 25%, Human race
- 20.5%, Place of birth, home, family
- 0%, Hometown, school

10. What is more important for happiness?

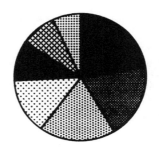

- 22.4%, Friends
- 19%, Marriage
- 19%, Personal character
- 13.8%, Job
- 10.3%, Love of parents
- 8.6%, Opportunity
- 6.9%, Order in one's country

11. What scares you the most?

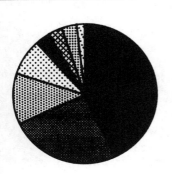

- 43.3%, Death of parents
- 25%, World war
- 11.7%, Totalitarian regime
- 8.3%, Enviromental disaaster
- 3.3%, Bad accident
- 3.3%, Sickness
- 3.3%, Not finding a job
- 1.6%, Crime
- 0%, Bad grades

255

12. If you had a magic wish, what would you wish for?

This last question was answered by 35 out of 43 students in the following way:

— I want to find all my relatives
— To become immortal
— To achieve all the set goals
— To develop spiritually (not religiously)
— To have a normal, happy life (with no wars, political infighting, orders from above); human life
— To have freedom in all aspects of my actions
— To have a happy life, to leave a good mark behind
— To live independently and vigorously, surrounded by good friends
— I want to be happy! And to have kids
— I don't want to be sorry about a purposelessly spent life
— Is it possible to formulate a most important desire
— To have a good life
— I want to contribute to building and fixing up of a new Russia
— To have humane and natural life in harmony with each other
— To see a rebirth of faith and re-establishment of order in Russia
— To be happy – to have many children, a good job, independence
— To do good deeds and through that to achieve happiness
— To be happy
— To have a secure future
— I want to have more happy people around me
— To see all my wishes come true
— To have such a life as not to be sorry of the wasted years
— To have a good life in all of its aspects
— To be happy in a happy Russia
— To preserve all that is good about my country
— To reach the highest level of education
— I want to develop a good personality in a full meaning of this word
— I want people to love one another and to love Russia
— I want to lead a long and interesting life
— To see people be kinder among themselves, toward nature and the world; to approach an ideal of Love
— To be healthy and happy
— To have a life which is not empty
— To see Russia become an autocratic monarchy
— To continue striving, to fight entropy, to be truly existential
— I want to see the end of the dissolution of Russia; life would be better for all of us

256

RUSSIA

AT THE CROSSROADS

REVIEW

"Russia at the Crossroads"

The following article presents an analysis of the essays collected in this book, in conjunction with the results of the survey. Forty three students participated in the contest, representing about .5% of eligible participants. Since this was not a random sampling, it cannot be held to be representative of the whole spectrum of the young Russian generation. However, it does represent a sample of the thinking, active part of that generation – of those, who are more likely to produce the cultural leaders of the future.

While all of the essays share the same principle topic, they vary widely in style, including philosophical essays (Shmakov, Holina), a dream (Trubitsina), the diary of a ship's ghost (Bandakov), a letter to a sister (Grigoryeva), a time-machine voyage (Lapshin), a story of Vityaz (a symbolic, mythical warrior figure), and autobiographies (Orlov, Tetelkin). They also vary in content – some choosing to examine a particular topic (e.g. the issue of land ownership by Dobrohotov), while others develop a whole historical/philosophical system of thought (Holina).

There are also a great number of similarities that emerge upon reading the essays: in the students' analyses of the topics of Russian history, in the direction of their attention toward certain events, and in their attitudes toward the present and the future.

In our analysis of the essays we can also use the results of the survey to help us to paint a clearer picture of the mindset of these authors.

To begin, it can be said that all of the authors seem to be unanimous in their negative view of the present, and in the commonly held conviction that Russia, as a country and a cultural entity, is facing great danger.

"... Our people have lost their national self-conscious, their trust in themselves and the future; physically undermined by gigantic losses: the hunger of the past years, alcoholism."

Irina Trubitsina

"... Indeed, life is not sweet for Russia right now."

Kseniya Holina

"Russia... Great country, Great Russian people, Great Russian culture. But all of this lies in the past, and will probably never be resurrected."

Dmitry Chegin

"Look around for yourself. We are on our way, not only to a full economic collapse, but headed towards moral degradation as well. On the streets I see embittered, tired-out faces. Doesn't it seem to you that people are slowly turning into beasts?"

Irina Grigoryeva

"Here they are, the signs of our times: growing poverty, crime and robbery; bankruptcy; massive waves of political murder, which remain largely uninvestigated; "civilized" rogues, whose symbols have become rubber chewing gum and rubber billy-clubs; frenzied struggles for power, which are really just for a higher standard of living; and, also, endless numbers of refugees, refugees..."

Sergey Marinin

In their attempts to explain and to justify the present situation and to find solutions and ways out, the authors naturally look to the past. Many of them see the roots of the Russian problems in the historical and geographical features of Russia and shift responsibility to the outside world. They cite, for example, that Russia, consisting of the great Eurasian plain, was an easy target for invading armies. This point of view describes Russia as the victim of a long chain of circumstances, as a passive sleeping giant, called upon from time to time to undergo immense suffering on behalf of the civilized world. The statement that this suffering was not in vain, but undergone on behalf of the world is indicative of the Russian global outlook, examples of which we will see later.

One such major trial and achievement of Russia is the 300-year-long domination by, and eventual liberation from the Mongolian yoke, which began in 1237, with the invasion of Russia by Chengiz Khan.

"It seems to me that there exists no other nation in the world that has suffered and survived through as much as has Russia: one-hundred and seventy years of the Tartar-Mongol yoke did not break down our ancestors, did not stop their aspirations for freedom, and the multiple wars did not embitter the hearts of the peaceful farmers."

Irina Grigoryeva

"... but Russia stood strong and even though the Mongols won, they got trapped in the "gigantic spaciousness", they got tired of weak but stubborn resistance. Knowing how those who made it roamed over regions of Europe, we could guess that, if Russia had not slowed and weakened the "steppe people", the Czechs probably would not have endured, and what might have ensued, in the rest of Europe, lies beyond the limits of our imaginations. "

Mikhail Gushin

In the trials and suffering under Mongol rule, the authors find the "mission of Russia" – to save the world. Indeed, the fact that Russia survived that dark period as an intact culture leads some to find hope in the present and for the future.

"But is it all that horrible in Russia? Did she not survive the Mongol-Tartar yoke, destroy it, and rebuild her strength a few centuries ago?"

Irina Trubitsina

While some authors see the present problems as an inheritance of foreign domination and the influence it had on the Russian way of government, many simply state that Russia was always unlucky to have bad rulers.

"Poor, long-suffering Russia!... she was never lucky with her rulers. History seems to always place short-sighted, illiterate individuals, or bloodthirsty tyrants at the helm of the great ship of Russia."

Svetlana Glushaeva

"There never was, not ever in Russia, a just power."

Egor Vereshagin

This approach is again significant in that it lays the blame with outside circumstances, as if the Russian people had no say, nor anything to do with their rulers.

Speaking of rulers, a majority of the writers give their approval to Peter The Great, whose reforms and military victories made Russia a world power.

"The captain (it was Peter) said, "If we want to live, we must modernize the ship." He gathered the people together and gave the orders to begin. The new snow-white sails were raised on the oaken masts, the cannons glittered in the sun. The ship became even greater and they sailed onward, proud of its power, showing itself in foreign ports. There was a great battle near one port with another huge vessel, but our ship stood firm and won its glory."

Pavel Bandakov

262

"You know, Marina, I wish I had lived at the time of Peter the Great. I admire the sharp mind, tact, and political flexibility of his man. During his rule, the stature of Russia had been raised o an unprecedented height. Foreign countries found out how owerful Russia could be. It was the era when "... With a sideways glance, other peoples and states step aside and yield the ath to her.""

Irina Grigoryeva

"... Peter I had little chance of becoming Czar. He was the ourteenth child of the Czar Aleksey Mikhailovich. Nevertheless, it was the fate of Russia to be ruled by this man.
It was a rare, and perhaps unique, case when Russia moved rom the dead point and took the path oriented to the West. Peter chose that road and went down it, destroying everything in is path. In an unbelievably short period, he built a navy and trengthened the army. He allowed for upward mobility. Russia achieved an access to the sea, the youth attended European universities, and beautiful St. Petersburg arose from he swamps."

Elizaveta Tuhsanova

"Before us stands "the great persona", a man whom many istorians place at the fore of Russian rulers. Before us – Peter he First. In only a quarter-century he was able to radically hange all of Russian life and send her along the most appropriate path of development for those times."

Sergey Lapshin

The survey results echo the essays in this instance, with 50% of the students preferring Peter The Great (See Q. 5 of the survey). The only other significant political leader to carry favor with the students being P.A. Stolypin (see essay by Dobrohotov). Both of these figures are viewed as strong, reformist leaders, who held the reins of power with a strong hand, while leading Russia down the path of progress. While many see the negative sides of Peter's forced reforms (Vereshagin, Tuhsanova, Lapshin), they accept the sacrifices as necessary and none even mention the fact that Peter strengthened the system of serfdom.

It is not surprising then that strong leadership is the most popular answer to the improvement of the state of affairs in Russia among the students (See Q.8 of the survey). This longing for a strong, powerful leader is closely connected with the major emotion which students express toward the future – hope. Such a passive attitude is an inheritance from the long history of Russia and from communism, where personal initiative was not welcomed.

In general, the students view the outside world almost exclusively as the western world, exhibiting a historical complex of inferiority. The mission of Russia becomes one of the savior of that civilization, starting with the protection of Europe from the Mongol hordes and continuing in more recent history as a counterbalance to the destructive forces within Europe itself. It is in this light that students view Russian victories over Napoleon and Hitler.

"How many times has Russia saved the world? At least twice: two invasions drowned in Russia, two wars – 1812 and the Second World War... "

"The Tartar-Mongol invasion? ... Russia stood strong and even though the Mongols won, they got trapped in the "gigantic spaciousness", they got tired of weak but stubborn resistance. Knowing how those who made it roamed over regions of Europe, we could guess that, if Russia had not slowed and weakened the "steppe people", the Czechs probably would not have endured, and what might have ensued, in the rest of Europe, lies beyond the limits of our imaginations."

Mikhail Gushin

"Who knows if, without this single faith, Russia would have been able to survive the Tartar-Mongol yoke, and stand as a buffer between wild Asia and developing Europe for three hundred years."

Elizaveta Tuhsanova

Having established all the suffering and sacrifices that Russia underwent on the behalf of the world, many come to a conclusion of the uniqueness of Russia's historical mission and see in Russia an ability to save the world yet again. And it does not matter that the world does not necessarily care to be saved – the fulfillment of Russia's mission is what counts.

"From the depths of the centuries, there arose a vague understanding of Russia's global mission. Russia was destined to fill the gap between all cultures by coming into direct contact with them, making it possible, a few centuries later, to deliver that highest truth for which this great country was created."

Kseniya Holina

This brings us to modern history, in particular - to the historical experiment of communism, which the country has just completed conducting on itself. While the students overwhelmingly reject the communist doctrine and see the present problems arising from the last seventy years, they still see it as another proof of Russian self-sacrifice for the sake of the world.

"For how long now have we been showing the world how not to live. We sacrificed ourselves to show to all the mistakes of historical development; so that others would be able to avoid them."

Mikhail Gushin

The students overwhelmingly view the Communist revolution as a national tragedy, perhaps a harshest test that history has imposed on Russia.

"For me, 1917 was scary because it attempted to crush that which was most sacred of the Russian genotype. Power took those who chose not to remember their roots, or as it says in the

Bible, prodigal sons. They destroyed the creative impulse of Russia because they could only destroy."

Vasily Orlov

"And then God's punishment came – Bolshevik rule began. What ensued was such that the period of provisional government seemed a paradise, to many, in comparison. Executions, murders, Cheka ("the extraordinary commission", i.e. the secret police), robberies... "

Dmitry Chegin

But while these writers reject communism, they lament the fall of the Soviet Union, the broken economic and political ties, the loss of superpower status. In their answer to Question 7 of the survey – *What do you think about the break-up of the USSR?* – the most popular answer is a negative one. Quotes from the students support this survey result.

"These reforms did not lead to anything but a deep economic crisis. The bureaucracy remained the same, while the form of government simply changed its name. . . And why was it decided that, with the car stuck in the mud, it would be easier to get out if the engine, wheels, and body were scattered in different directions?"

Sergey Lapshin

"The heart shrinks when looking at the thick lines of borders on the map, which split up the various republics. The separa-

tions of the Ukraine and Belorussia seem to be especially ab-surd."

Mikhail Ezhov

One gets a sense that there was a kind of comfort before, in the era of economic stability, well defined social roles, and the presence of a government as a leader and teacher. They miss the security of Mother Russia's bosom, having undergone in their short lives total loss of certainty. This is probably why they put such a strong emphasis on family in defining themselves, and what scares them most is the death of their parents (See Questions 3 and 11 of the survey).

It is this loss of certainty that makes others turn to Russia's history in the attempt to find a cornerstone of their identity. But the body of history is so vast that it can provide supporting evidence to a large variety of views, sometimes quite opposite.

"We will take this risk of stating that the history of Russia has three cycles, which would be as follow: 1. Sedition, 2. The Ditch, 3. Stagnation. There is sedition in Russia now. . ."

Dmitry Shmakov

"For Russia, the day before yesterday was good, therefore tomorrow will be good as well because near-sighted politicians will not be able to destroy the Russian national memory."

Vasily Orlov

While history provides them with few certain answers, what unites them all is the view of the present. The dominant feeling of the writers description of today is the feeling of being at a crossroads.

"*And now, this great, millions-strong Russian superpower, and centuries-old cultural tradition, is again faced with a choice of historic proportions... Where to... , who will Russia follow? This question painfully confronts government and the society as a whole, since the choice of the path of development embodies great risk in its direct consequences, which are matters of life and death.*"

Yuliya Bak

Elizaveta Tuhsanova in her essay describes Vityaz, an ancient warrior, standing at the crossroads, as a symbol of Russia. As he tries to see what is in front of him, he sees just an endless steppe, not finding any clear answers to his questions.

"*Yes, it is hard to sort out what is going on today in Russia and, what is most important, is... what lies underfoot... road or swamp?*
Vityaz squints his eyes to see further, beyond the horizon, to grasp what lies ahead. But he can only make out a large stone, marking yet another crossroads on the endless steppe, which merges with the cold, grey sky."

Elizaveta Tuhsanova

The feeling of uncertainty bears heavily on these young minds. One author even writes with some envy of the previous generation, who would have had well-defined answers, prescribed by official ideology, were they to have been faced with the task of writing a similar essay.

"Our parents would have most likely drawn a breath of relief had they been asked to write such an essay at their final school examinations; back then everyone was proud of the homeland, she was universally loved, because, since the compulsory days of Oktyabryata, they had known:

'Oh, how wide my native country is,
There are abundant woods, fields, and rivers,
I know of no other country,
Where man draws freedom with every breath.'"[1]

Sergey Marinin

The rejection of communism and feelings of uncertainty in the essays combine with an almost unanimous critical attitude toward the present reality. This is the topic where we hear the most emotional, passionate voices of the writers. They criticize politicians and intellectuals, they deplore the economic situation and general decline of morality. Some go as far as rejecting the very people and their traditions.

"O Great Russian Impasse! How many talents have you ruined? How many loving people have stumbled over you? This

---

[1] Soviet classic song

impasse is created not so much by the government as by the masses."

Egor Vereshagin

"The years passed... All that our people went through now seems like a bad dream, but today – it is the same horror, the same black and impenetrable darkness. We are bogged down in the details of everyday life, petrified, indifferent, ... truly, we are the same frightened people"

Svetlana Glushaeva

"Our people have lost their national self-consciousness, their trust in themselves and the future; physically undermined by gigantic losses: the hunger of the past years, alcoholism."

Irina Trubitsina

"To tell you the truth, I feel pain when I think of our country. Look around for yourself. We are on our way, not only to a full economic collapse, but headed towards moral degradation as well. On the streets I see embittered, tired-out faces. Doesn't it seem to you that people are slowly turning into beasts?"

Irina Grigoryeva

"Russia is dominated right now by economic, political, and, most of all, spiritual crises. The Russian soul is in a state of chaos, veiled in clouds of smoke."

Dmitry Shmakov

With one exception (Dmitry Chegin), they criticize the war in Chechnya, which was at its very beginning when they wrote their compositions.

"The war in Chechnya shows that to fight one's own people is the last thing to do. In national relations within the country, there is a need to return to a healthy imperial practice which presupposes full (true, and not ostentatious) freedom of self-government."

Mikhail Ezhov

"Now Russia is going through a new crisis: the war in Chechnya, which is strikingly similar to the Afghan situation. The decision for the deployment of troops was made by a small group of officials and the president, with the consent of the parliament. ... our soldiers have become hostages because of the incompetent actions of their leadership who sent first year draftees into this "meat grinder". On the whole, events in Chechnya give a very bad impression."

Aleksey Podnebesny

A majority of the students reject the recent past and the choices made by the previous generations. They find their country in a deep crisis engulfing all spheres of life and they are uncertain of the direction their country is taking. One would expect gloomy and pessimistic predictions from these authors concerning the future of their country and a cautious and pragmatic approach toward their personal choices regarding their livelihood. It is here, in their attitudes toward the future that the

272

fate of this upcoming generation is revealed; as is, consequently, that which lies ahead for Russia. This is the key to understanding and seeing these young people as individuals, with their own original thoughts, for writing about the future requires more than mere observations of the present and repetition of the input they have received of recent and ancient historical facts.

(Incidentally, it is also interesting to examine where this input comes from? Question 3 of the survey shows that the students give their preference to four choices to the question *What had the most influence on your view of the world?* in the following order: Family – 40.4%, Books – 34.6%, Friends – 17.3%, School – 7.7%. Family being first seems to exhibit a quite common human characteristic. Books being second is probably an indicative characteristic of the group as writers and most likely could be substituted by TV for the average member of their generation. The fact that school ranks last, however, could represent a strong aversion to institutions.)

On the whole, students spent only an unexpectedly minimal amount of their essays writing about the future. The table below shows the relative number of pages spent on covering these eras in their essays.

	Past	Present	Future
Relative % of essays dedicated to covering an era	63%	30%	7%

The numbers are even more revealing if we take into account the fact that 6 of the writers, representing 30%, contribute more than 70% to covering the future. Therefore, the majority of the writers (14 out of 20) spend less than 4% writing about that era which, it seems, should be the one of utmost importance and concern to them.

Upon reading all 20 essays there emerge three common themes, which almost all of the writers seem to subscribe to. The first group exhibits a *hope against logic* attitude, lacking any clear conclusions on the future. The second group is characterized by a more realistic approach and thorough analysis, and is pessimistic in their view of the future. The third and final group can be described as individuals willing to assume personal responsibility for the future of Russia.

The first group, which comprises most of the writers, describes the tragedy of Russian history and the horrors of the present situation, and readily acknowledges the fact that they are not certain of what will happen to Russia in the future.

"Only prophets and insane people can see the future."

Egor Vereshagin

"I do not know what "tomorrow" will be like. I hope it will be a happy one."

Evgeny Tetelkin

This argument seems to provide a justification not to dwell on the subject much longer, and they finish their essays, while expressing a vague hope for the future. In a way, they seem frightened of the future, facing it with only unfounded hope. Deep down, they seem to understand the logical inconsistency of such a historical approach, repeatedly quoting famous lines by Tyutchev (... *By mind alone – not to be known*), and by Gogol (... *Where are you racing to?*). In doing so, they join the traditions of many previous generations, who existed on promises and hopes for a radiant future for many a century.

"Russia is always under way, always trying to reach some goal. It seems to have arrived... Just a bit more and it would be there, but already another beckons from a different direction... Life in expectation of something far distant, so ideal that it is unimaginable... How many names that distant goal has had – glorious future, heavenly Jerusalem... "

Mikhail Gushin

The idea of Russian uniqueness and their subsequent defiance of common reason as applied to Russian history allows some of them to let their fantasy reign free and to come up with some rather far-fetched scenarios, prophesying the salvation of the world by Russia.

"I think that our culture will still be reborn. I have even made-up a name for this era – "the Second Renaissance". No, think about it... listen to the beauty in these words... "the second renaissance"! These words will sound literally all over the world, not in Italian, but in Russian – 'Vtoroe Vozrozhdenie'".

Egor Vereshagin

"... Russia will discover and implement a new religion, new teachings built on the doctrines of the past and those of moder-

275

*nity, a new view of world order. She will enrich other cultures through her experience. She will deliver a highest truth for which she has been being prepared for over many centuries..." *

Kseniya Holina

Everything changes, everything stays the same... While the essays of the students illustrate to us the impact of recent changes which are taking place in Russian society, they also underscore the ever-present characteristics of the Russian character, of the Russian soul... Vera, Nadezhda, Lyubov' — these are three ancient Russian names, which are often remembered together in the exact order. They translate as Faith, Hope, Love... And this is exactly what these essays consist of: Faith in their country despite the past and present hardships, Hope for the future and ever-present all-engulfing Love of their motherland and the world.

The second group of writers represented a pessimistic outlook, based on their analysis of the past. This group of consists of four writers: Gushin, Tuhsanova, Chernevsky and Shmakov. While Chernevsky provides one of the most thorough political and economic analyses of the future, which leads him to conclude that Russia's fate is to become a half-colony of the major post-industrial world powers, Tuhsanova seems to be unable to reconcile the paradoxes of Russia's history.

"Therefore, we will most likely become a half-colony from which there will be a cheap import of all natural resources,

which will be maintained for the purposes of international security at a level just above poverty. "

Artyom Chernevsky

"But the people, it seems, have been forgotten once again. They are loosing their trust in their leaders. They are confused by much of what is going on around them. Vityaz, himself, is unclear about many things. He cannot even tell where Russia ends these days. For example, Chechnya, ... is it Russia?

Yes, it is hard to sort out what is going on today in Russia and, what is most important, is... what lies underfoot... road or swamp?

Vityaz squints his eyes to see further, beyond the horizon, to grasp what lies ahead. But he can only make out a large stone, marking yet another crossroads on the endless steppe, which merges with the cold, grey sky."

Elizaveta Tuhsanova

Gushin and Shmakov, on the other hand, concentrate their attention on the study of the phenomenon of Russian character, the Russian soul, if you will. In their essays, which, in our opinion, are among the best, they study the historical and philosophical aspects of the Russian soul and come up with some sobering conclusions. After a thorough and well-argued study of the phenomenon, they go further than simply stating their inability to tackle the issue of Russia's future. Their predictions are decidedly pessimistic. It is a pity that the two authors who undertook the most comprehensive study of Russian character, are not able to find any hope within themselves or their history.

These two essays are merited with an incredible intellectual honesty and seem to shed more light on the theme of *Russia: Yesterday, Today, Tomorrow* than the majority with their rather superficial *hope despite logic* approach to the future.

Both authors start by placing the theme of the essay in historical context. While Gushin states after L. Gumilev that Russia as a cultural entity is at the end of its life cycle and that rebirth is simply impossible, Shmakov immediately puts forth a thesis that the history of his native country consists but of three components: *sedition, the ditch and stagnation.* After these openings, they attempt to find the reasons for these conditions, and this, in turn, leads them to eternal discontent, uncertainty and anarchy, which are major aspects of the Russian Soul.

"The Russian soul is in a state of chaos, veiled in clouds of smoke. Its mystery remains impenetrable even to Russians."

Dmitry Shmakov

"The people of Russia are phenomenally apolitical. The full anarchy of these people has been carried throughout our history. There is no other such anarchy in any country, as that of Russia (this is one thing we can be proud of)."

Mikhail Gushin

The statements above point to another historical trait of the Russian character – the explosive mixture of humility and pride, the eternal duality and uncertainty of Russian nature. For even though they do not see a very bright and glorious future on the horizon, both Gushin and Shmakov are absolutely certain of

ussia's uniqueness and greatness. Describing the messianic
earch of Russia, they point to the duality of its national charac-
er. While Shmakov defines the two antagonistic sides, Gushin
hooses to put forth two scenarios in the form of a question.

*"In the Russian's soul there is a struggle between two super-
deas which determine the meaning and content of all other ideas:
'erun (pre-Christian Russian god) and God. If for some time
ae cult of the wild forces of nature predominate, man worships
ae Beast; when the higher forces triumph, man worships the
reator. Paganism and Christianity go hand in hand in Russian
fe, mixing and intertwining, and simultaneously resisting each
ther... "*

Dmitry Shmakov

*"Were the philosophers wrong, then, in thinking that a renais-
ance of the Great Russia would save the world? Is it possible
aat Russia might wilt before fulfilling its mission, a mission that
ould then remain undiscovered?...
Indeed, have we failed to fulfill one great mission while taking
n another – left to us from above, so we would not be insulted?
or how long now have we been showing the world how not to
ve. We sacrificed ourselves to show to all the mistakes of his-
rical development; so that others would be able to avoid them.
re we to become the new Christ, come to save humanity?
laybe this is the second coming? Russia the great Jesus?...
'oly One?... "*

Mikhail Gushin

The duality of Russian nature leads to anarchy, to the loss of order. Uncertainty reins and two opposing forces cannot reconcile their differences.

"There is another love of the Russian people – the genetic love of VOLYA. An analogical concept to VOLYA does not exist anywhere else. It is not possible, even in Russian, to explain this idea. It can only be felt. What is VOLYA? ...sleep on as long as you like, drink by the bottle, take off riding at high speed... ("What Russian does not like a fast ride?" – Gogol) ... to drink into stupor, to fly! To get a monthly stipend and spend it all, not caring that you will suffer for the next month...

Ach! Swing from the shoulder! Let fly my hand! Go wild, soul! ... to the mother anarchy!"

Mikhail Gushin

"From the point of view of social human rights norms, Russia is populated with barbarians. These Russian barbarians have two curses: "... below is the power of darkness, above is the darkness of power."

Dmitry Shmakov

Having diagnosed their country with a disease of eternal disorder, these authors are also convinced that the patient has no chance of recovery. They end their essays differently, while agreeing on poor prospects for the future.

"However, it is fruitless and meaningless to build illusions about the future, since it does not exist in reality, as does not the

280

past – only the present exists, and man wants to change it, to build a heaven on earth. But utopias spring up from inability to sort out the present...

There is a recurrent sedition in Russia now... The prediction of the future seems to be an ungrateful undertaking. "Collapse" has happened. There is nothing new in sight which is able to move us from this standstill. It is not clear which idea will conquer our minds and hearts and determine our future path...

"Russia, where are you racing to? Answer me! There is no answer. The bells are tinkling and filling the air with their wonderful pealing; the air is torn and thundering as it turns to wind; everything on earth comes flying past and, looking askance at her, other peoples and states move aside and make way." Nikolai Gogol"

Dmitry Shmakov

"Russia, where are they all pulling you to? Some to capitalism, to the market. Others to communism. They pulled you to one side. Then the others came and said we were pulling in the wrong way... And Russia is still the same as it was one thousand years ago. The people never became citizens. They sleep ... just as this idyllic, quiet city cares not which way we will choose now, as long as it exists... And maybe this is the mysterious Russian soul?"

Mikhail Gushin

It is not surprising that both authors end their essays with questions, as if admitting that the realm of human logic and language can not provide answers to the mystery of Russia. This seems to be a widely held opinion among the majority of essayists who often use the following quote by Tyutchev:

By mind alone - not to be known,
By common yardstick - not to be measured,
She has her own, special way,
In Russia you must simply trust.

While many of the previously discussed writers do not seem to need to justify their hope, a few writers base their hope for the future on their own readiness to accept the responsibility of their generation personally.

"All of Russian history is a ship moving through the oceans of life and time. These oceans have strong currents and stormy winds. Whether or not our ship will prevail, depends on us. My only desire and goal is: to be happy in a happy Russia. So, grant me God, that the majority of our generation should have the goal of seeing Russia happy, of dedicating our lives to her. We trust Russia will be resurrected!"

Pavel Bandakov

The above quote serves as a link to this third group of essayists, whose approach in dealing with the future consists of emphasizing personal responsibility and self-reliance.

"It is up to our choice and our actions, to determine whether the sun will rise over the Russian Empire, our whether the cold night will descend."

Aleksey Podnebesny

As the above quote illustrates, not all of the authors who subscribe to responsibility and self-reliance are over-aboundly optimistic. They seem to be more sober-minded than the first group as if overwhelmed by the enormity of the task before them.

"Russia awaits help. What will stop our free-fall? Who will prevent the death of Great Russia, that living organism containing the lives of our ancestors of the preceding millennia? So what is the reason for all our misfortunes? It is not simple to answer these questions... Our salvation will not come before our acknowledgment and understanding of the danger – an understanding that must be shared by all. It is necessary to see this truth in all its nakedness; to look this hard reality in the eyes. It is especially important to mobilize, for the defense of Russia, all healthy, well-intentioned forces of society. Only if we can avoid these cataclysms, will we be able to speak of the prospects of our country's rebirth; about the ways in which we will find contentedness and peace; and a life of dignity and great goals."

Mikhail Ezhov

While this group comprises only 25% of the writers, it is indicative of the positive changes which are taking place in Russian society, where only a generation ago almost everyone worked for the one and only boss – the State. Vasily Orlov, who adheres to both themes of responsibility and hope, bases his optimism on "Russian creative impulse and a holy faith in the future of Russia". He further states:

"I accept my past as it was, but I want to build the future myself, in such a way as to not ashame my grandparents or my great grandparents or my descendants."

Vasily Orlov

The winners of the contest, Vasily Orlov and Evgeny Tetelkin, both dedicate their essays to writing about their families. Tetelkin writes of three generations of his family undergoing the migration from Tashkent, Uzbekistan to Nizhny Novgorod, Russia during the era of late perestroika and the break-up of the Soviet Union. Orlov focuses his attention on the heritage of his family, finding himself a descendant of both communist and capitalist traditions. Yet, he sees a unifying basis in both of them – a creative impulse, which continues to be passed from generation to generation. This affirmation of family traditions and readiness to face the task of building the future within the framework of a multigenerational moral code might give one a reason for guarded optimism about Russia's future. Is this an indication of young sprouts making it to the sun through the rubble of communist ideology? Are they just expressing the optimism and hunger for action common to their age group? Either way, they express common sense and that alone makes them valuable to the future of their country.

We have attempted to organize and underscore the major themes of the essays contained in this book. Now, in conclusion, we turn from what the essayists expressed in their writing and how they did so, and look at this body of work in a historical context, asking the question of what do these essays tell us about the essence of the Russian soul and, consequently, of Russia's future.

> "... And an eternal battle,
> We only dream of peace... "
> Alexander Blok

While the above quote by a Russian turn-of-the-century poet, who lived to embrace the Revolution, only to be gravely disappointed and to die soon thereafter, could be applied to life itself, with varying degrees of generality, it is his native country that it describes in the poem "Kulikovskoe Pole". We propose that Russia is a country on an eternal search, internally unstable, because of irreconcilable contradictions which are that much harder to resolve, having become an integral part of the Russian character itself.

The contradictions which make up the Russian character are too numerous to list, but many could be derived from its geographical location on the plains between Europe and Asia. Russia served as a battlefield for invading armies from the East and the West. (A common Russian saying states... "scratch a Russian and you will find a Tartar.") The country's royalty and nobility originated from the Viking family of Rurik, who came

285

to rule Novgorod in 862, and continued through Ivan The Terrible (1533-1584), the last of that lineage among Russia's rulers. From 1237 to 1480 Russia was under the Mongolian yoke. Therefore, western *and* eastern ways of life became the foundations of Russian character. On the other hand, spiritual traditions are also affected by this division. From the struggle between paganism and Christianity to the Raskol (major schism within the Russian Orthodox Church, persisting today, initiated when Nikon became a patriarch in 1652), Russia has been torn by religious strife.

The historical behavior of Russians is also full of contradictions – from long periods of slavery and serfdom to bursts of revolution and turmoil. Also, Russia's greatest quests in the expansion of its geographical borders and in the establishment of a world stature were made under the leadership of the monarchs who were the most cruel and authoritarian, as in the case of Ivan the Terrible, Peter the Great, and Stalin, whereas the reformist czar Alexander II, who ended serfdom in 1861, was assassinated by the revolutionaries.

Despite centuries of turmoil, tyranny, and social experimentation, and an apparent present desire for stability and certainty, the inherited underlying contradictions of its nature and the persistence of messianic ideals retain a propensity for dangerous cataclysm. It is as if Russia is always searching, as if trying to build a great Babylonian tower. The Bible tells us that there is a great price to pay for such undertakings. The price of knowledge of Good and Evil is the exile from Heaven. But Russia continues in its myth of Syziphus. Is Russia ready to pay a terrible price again? Only time can answer this question.

Conclusion

"Intelligentsia as an Expression
of Russia's Quest"

"I, Vasily Orlov, 16 years old, put truly Russian questions to myself: "Who is to blame?" and "What is to be done?" I understand well that, for the last two hundred years, our national thought has not found resolutions to them, finding only dead ends or bloody answers."

The above quote holds a key to understanding the phenomenon of Russian intelligentsia.* The intelligentsia is a rather unique class of people who are united not by social and/or economic factors, but by their real or imaginary sense of belonging to the class of the creators of culture, of contributors to progress, of people dedicated to resolving the injustice present in this world, of people whose very goal is an improvement of life itself. This idealistic and romantic approach to reality has demonstrated at times a strength of faith on the order of religious

---

This book places special emphasis and concern on the concept and term intelligentsia", particularly in this concluding article, and in the essays by Dmitry Chegin and Svetlana Glushaeva. Intelligentsia is presented in a broader sense than the English literal convention of "the intelligentsia", taken to denote a specific social stratum of Russian society. This publication considers it to be of utmost importance to bring to bear that intelligentsia signifies a number of other concepts, such as a particular evolving self-consciousness, as well as a facet and mindset of Russian culture itself. Further aspects of intelligentsia are also dealt with in the articles, which further reveals the complex nature of this idea in Russian ideology. Hence, other notions of intelligentsia will herein be differentiated from simple reference to the social group in that the latter will be referred to, as in customary English, as "the intelligentsia".

martyrdom, without the discipline or logical inner consistency of a major religion. While the number of answers to the above questions varied over the course of a couple of centuries with varying degrees of consensus, it is the questions, not the answers, which define and exemplify the major search of the intelligentsia, and, consequently, intelligentsia itself.

As a result of Peter the Great's "chopping through a window to Europe", Russia found itself face to face with Western civilization. At that point in history, Russia was an underdeveloped giant with a long history of authoritarianism, stuck, in a way, in the Middle Ages. Peter could force Russia to become a naval power, a major military force and so on, he could even build a wonderful imperial European city in place of a swamp. But he could not make Russia undergo a renaissance – that, the culture had to do it on its own. Through the *axed window,* with Peter's encouragement, came foreigners (mostly Germans, Poles, and Italians), while young Russians went to the Western universities and trade schools. The unavoidable comparison between realities of life at home and in the West created a certain complex of inferiority among the newly educated Russian elite. It is not surprising that one of the first major philosophical works – *First Letter on the Philosophy of History* (1826) by Chaadaev, argues the point that Russia took a wrong turn in history by rejecting Catholicism. At the same time, the success of Russian arms and global messianic ideas of the Russian Orthodox church, with its myth of Moscow being the Third Rome, provided Russian intellectuals with a sense of superiority. Add to that the feeling of being newly enlightened and you get a strange mixture of pride

nd humility, and ... a heroism of the newly converted, because
Western philosophical thought became a religion of the newly
ducated class. While the rediscovery of the Classics was a
major factor in the Renaissance in Europe, Russia discovered
ot only the Classics, but well-developed philosophical tradi-
ons dating from the times of Thomas Aquinas and Bacon to
ant and Hegel.

The newly educated class would have remained as such, never
ecoming intelligentsia, if it had not been for the *accursed ques-
ons* dealing with moral justice. Desiring to resolve obvious
justices of reality, some of the new prophets of what came to
e intelligentsia, came forward questioning the social and eco-
omic order of the country from the point of view of ideal
Western models, from Plato's "Republic" to Thomas Moor's
Utopia." The reaction of the authorities who prosecuted and
mprisoned "the philosophizers" provided intelligentsia with its
rst martyrs. Chaadaev was declared insane and placed under
ouse arrest, Hertsen was imprisoned and exiled...
ntelligentsia found itself in opposition and that confrontation
ith authorities became one of the defining factors of the very
lea of intelligentsia. There were other distinguishing factors as
ell.

It is hard to overestimate the importance of Peter the Great.
is deeds were sufficient example of his powers, but the effect
at he had on Russia far exceeds his time and epoch. His ex-
mple of challenging and changing reality at will became part of
Russian intelligent's psychological portrait. The result of
eter's revolution is a phenomenon of intelligentsia – a powerful

social stratum, whose goal is a practical transformation of the world toward the betterment of human kind.

Both questions quoted by Orlov, also called "accursed questions" were made famous by writers. This points to another characteristic of intelligentsia – global thinking. Religion and philosophy alone were too narrow to satisfy the Russian intellectual. It is literature which became a genre which could encompass all of the methods of human thought and feelings. Hertsen's novel *Who is to blame?* (1841-45) helped to define a feeling which was prevalent among intelligentsia faced with the shortcomings of reality. The question illustrates an attitude of obvious discontent with a status quo and turns attention toward finding those responsible. Chernyshevsky's *What is to be done?* (1863) poses a second fundamental question of intelligentsia. In the novel he suggests a few answers ranging from *rational egoism* to the portrayal of a *super-hero revolutionary*. Lenin would later redefine the answer, calling for power through the actions of a few thousand fanatical revolutionaries and finding the place to lay blame – imperialism and capitalism.

The resolutions and answers to the above questions defined the major search of intelligentsia, which resulted, after a long and heroic struggle, in the overthrow of social order and the seizure of power by the communists, who took and established power through mass terror. Intelligentsia became one of the main targets of the communists, who had no need anymore for anybody daring to ask *the accursed questions*. By then, intelligentsia was a broader social class, of which the revolutionary movement was but a small part, but the most politically active and decisive, in Peter's tradition. But, if Peter's main impulse vas a creative and realistic one, the new rulers who renamed St. Petersburg to Leningrad were building a utopia by the most tyrannical and repressive means. Therefore, the search of intelligentsia and its attempts to reform the world according to an ideal model of a just society ended in almost total failure and almost total physical annihilation of intelligentsia as such.

The period following the death of Stalin and the end of mass terror witnessed a rebirth of intelligentsia and the accursed questions. And again the first question put her on the path of direct confrontation with the authorities, with persecutions and martyrs to follow. But it seems that intelligentsia had learned some lessons of history and one of the main points of contention with the rulers became the right of asking the questions at all, and the struggle became one for Human Rights. The shift from a global, to a local approach to reality did not stop the authorities from waging a campaign of severe persecution against dissidents, which they seemed to have won by the early eighties. Then came perestroika, the fall of the communist order and post-communism.

And now, the accursed questions are being asked yet again. While the young writers who wrote these essays can not speak for all of intelligentsia, they nevertheless are indicative of the answers which are prevalent in Russia now. So, how do they answer those questions and what similarities and differences do they have as compared with previous generations?

The majority of the writers seem to agree with their predecessors in finding the society in which they live in deep crisis. But even though they are quick to blame, their blame is addressed so diversely that it is hard to find a consensus among them. They range from geographical location, to the Mongol yoke, to present government, to Russian national character, and to intelligentsia itself. It is in the totality of their blame that we find an echo of the global approach of their intellectual forefathers. But one of the major differences is the lack of focus on a specific scapegoat, be it communists or capitalists. It seems that as they inherited the search for someone to blame, they lost the focus of hatred and the belief that a negative approach can bring about the resolutions of society's shortcomings. While it alone cannot be interpreted as a constructive force, the absence of hate is already an accomplishment in itself.

In analyzing the answers to the second question of what is to be done in the present situation, a majority of the essayists exhibit a great degree of uncertainty and timidity, hardly presenting any answers at all. The major group, the optimists, basically express hope in the fate of Mother Russia, while pessimists see no point in doing anything constructive in the land of lost hope. But it is those who call for action and who have a program of action who interest us the most in trying to see where the efforts of this young generation would be directed.

The common characteristic of those who tackle the question of what is to be done has to do with personal responsibility and self-reliance. And this is one of the most promising signs of the latest changes in Russia and one of the most distinguishing characteristics of this generation – having been disillusioned in the grand plans of previous generations, they turn to themselves, ready to assume personal responsibility for their country. And, paradoxically, it is those who turn their focus from global to local matters, who feel themselves as continuing the traditions of their forefathers, whom they associate with the best Russia has to offer.

With the advance of political freedoms in post-communist Russia, intelligentsia loses one of the factors which provided it with the intensity of a religious order - its martyrdom for the sake of Truth. *Accursed questions* lose their appeal of forbidden fruit and after public discussion, analyses are put on the back burner as front pages are filled with very real and important news, from Chechnya to miners' strikes. With Russia's integration into the world market, the sense of Russia's uniqueness is also being challenged in Russian minds. What we are witnessing now are the remaining days of intelligentsia as intellectuals are becoming more concerned with resolving problems on a local level, starting with themselves. Having failed in its gigantic victory over the old order, intelligentsia is disappearing, splitting up into different groups of professionals in the era of political openness and economic enterpreneurism. It seems that the question of *Who is to blame?* would soon be replaced with *What is the problem?* Again, this is an opinion derived from an analysis of the students who offer answers to *what is to be done?*

All of the above leads us to predict that with the advance of privatization, continuation of political freedoms and integration into the world community, intelligentsia as it was known will cease to exist, giving way to different political movements and local politics. This would, in turn, lead to a stabilization of society, with the new Russian generation of intellectuals changing the world around them by small, but real, steps. The time has been long due – only Russia can help Russia.

293

"My great great grandfather Dimity Perov, manager of the Morozov factory, and grandfather Osipov Anatoly Andreevich, Secretary of Komsomol Committee of the Gorky car plant, carried within them the Russian creative impulse and a holy faith in the future of Russia.

I, living at the end of the twentieth century, do not want to be their judge. I accept my past as it was, but I want to build the future myself, in such a way as to not shame my grandparents or my great grandparents or my descendants."

Vasily Orlov